D0788343

FREDERICK DOUGLASS

The African-American Biographies Series

—African-American Biographies—

FREDERICK DOUGLASS

Speaking Out Against Slavery

Series Consultant:
Dr. Russell L. Adams, Chairman
Department of Afro-American Studies, Howard University

Anne Schraff

Enslow Publishers, Inc.

40 Industrial Road   PO Box 38
Box 398   Aldershot
Berkeley Heights, NJ 07922   Hants GU12 6BP
USA   UK

http://www.enslow.com

Library of Congress Cataloging-in-Publication Data

Schraff, Anne E.
      Frederick Douglass : speaking out against slavery / Anne Schraff.
          p. cm. — (African-American biographies)
      Includes bibliographical references (p.   ) and index.
      ISBN 0-7660-1773-7 (hardcover)
      1. Douglass, Frederick, 1817?-1895—Juvenile literature. 2. African
American abolitionists—Biography—Juvenile literature. 3. Abolitionists—
United States—Biography—Juvenile literature. 4. Antislavery
movements—United States—History—19th century—Juvenile literature.
[1. Douglass, Frederick, 1817?-1895. 2. Abolitionists. 3. African
Americans—Biography. 4. Antislavery movements.] I. Title. II. Series.
E449.D75 S38   2001
973.8'092—dc21

                                            2001004470

Printed in the United States of America

10 9 8 7 6 5 4 3 2 1

To Our Readers:
We have done our best to make sure all Internet Addresses in this book were active
and appropriate when we went to press. However, the author and the publisher
have no control over and assume no liability for the material available on those
Internet sites or on other Web sites they may link to. Any comments or suggestions
can be sent by e-mail to comments@enslow.com or to the address on the back
cover.

Every effort has been made to locate all copyright holders of material used in this
book. If any errors or omissions have occurred, corrections will be made in future
editions of this book.

Illustration Credits: Courtesy, American Antiquarian Society, p. 43;
Illustrated by Christopher N. Schraff, p. 115; Library of Congress, pp. 6,
22, 30, 32, 39, 49, 51, 56, 61, 65(L), 65(R), 72, 75, 80, 83, 87, 89, 97, 112;
Missouri Historical Society, St. Louis, by Thomas Satterwhite Noble,
p. 15; National Archives, p. 9; National Park Service, Frederick Douglass
National Historic Site, pp. 95, 103, 111.

Cover Credit: Library of Congress

CONTENTS

Frederick Douglass (born Frederick Bailey)

1

"I WAS A MAN NOW"

n January 1, 1834, fifteen-year-old Frederick Bailey was, for the first time in his life, a field slave. Born into slavery, he had always served in homes. Now his master had rented him out to Edward Covey, a farmer on Maryland's Eastern Shore with a reputation as a slave-breaker. Covey was known as a man who could break the spirit of any rebellious slave.

On this very cold day Frederick was sent into the woods to get a load of wood that he had chopped and stacked the previous day. Frederick was ordered to drive an ox cart, something he had never done before.

Covey instructed him briefly, then sent him off. Disaster soon struck the inexperienced young man.

A sudden noise frightened the oxen and they took off, dragging the cart behind them, banging it against trees, and finally overturning it. Frederick struggled frantically to get the team disentangled from the brush. He righted the cart and finally reached the pile of wood. He began loading the logs into the cart, and when it was full he started for home. As he reached the Covey farm, the ox team once again bolted, breaking Covey's gate and almost crushing Frederick against the shattered wood.

When Covey learned of the accident and the long time Frederick had taken to do what Covey considered a minor job, he ordered the boy back into the woods at once. Frederick later recalled the incident in detail. Covey went to a large black gum tree, glared at the boy, and said, "I'll teach you how to waste time and break gates."[1] Using his jackknife, he cut off three shoots, or switches. "Take off your clothes," he told Frederick.[2] Frederick refused and Covey rushed at him, tore off his clothing, and flogged the boy. The whip cut deeply into Frederick's back, causing blood to run down his spine and raising welts as large as his little finger.[3]

It was only the beginning of what would be regular, brutal beatings at Covey's hands.

During one hot August day, Frederick and the other slaves were separating wheat from chaff.

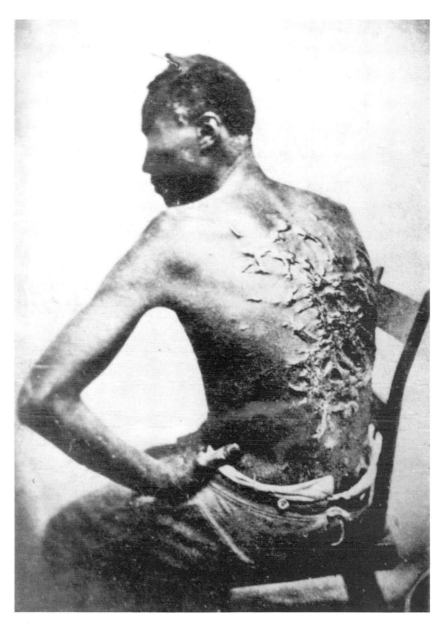

Their masters' brutal beatings often left slaves crisscrossed with scars.

Frederick was so exhausted by the long days, often working from sunup well into darkness, that he snatched a moment to rest. Covey found him and gave him a hard kick to his side. Frederick still refused to rise on command, so Covey snatched up a hickory slat, striking Frederick a sharp blow to the head.

With blood streaming "from the crown of my head to my feet," as Frederick remembered, he ran from the Covey farm to the home of his master.[4] When he told Thomas Auld, his master, of the cruel treatment he had been dealt, Auld was unmoved. He ordered Frederick back to Covey's farm.

The brutal treatment at the hands of Covey continued until one day when Covey tried once more to thrash Frederick. Frederick described how the "fighting madness" came upon him as he fought back against Covey.[5] Frederick grabbed Covey's throat and flung the man to the ground. When Covey called on nearby slaves to help him subdue Frederick, they pretended not to hear.

The battle between Frederick and Edward Covey raged for two hours. Frederick was not trying to hurt Covey, but he wanted to keep Covey from hurting him. Covey finally gave up the effort, telling Frederick, "Now, you scoundrel, go to your work!"[6] The humiliated Covey pretended that he had succeeded in humbling Frederick.

The teenaged Frederick was jubilant. He saw this

act of defiance as "the turning point in my career as a slave."[7] He changed after the fight. "I was *nothing* before," he said, "*I was a man* now."[8] He had reached the point where he was no longer afraid to die, and that gave him courage to stand up to Covey. During the final months that he worked for Covey, Frederick was never whipped again.

2

SOMEBODY'S CHILD

rederick Augustus Washington Bailey was born in February 1818 near Tuckahoe in Talbot County on the Eastern Shore of Maryland. According to legend, Tuckahoe gained its name when a local farmer took a hoe belonging to another man. "Took a hoe" became Tuckahoe.

Frederick's mother was Harriet Bailey, daughter of Isaac Bailey, a free black man, and Betsy Bailey, a copper-dark slave. Betsy Bailey had five daughters: Jenny, Esther, Milly, Priscilla, and Harriet. According to law, all Betsy's children became slaves like their mother and were the property of their mother's master.

Frederick did not know who his father was, but he always believed that his father was a white man. "He was admitted to be such," Frederick later wrote, "by all I ever heard speak of my parentage."[1] As a small boy, and all through his life, Frederick wondered who his father might be. He always noticed that his skin color, slightly yellowish, was different from the color of his siblings, and that fueled his conviction that his father was white.[2]

Soon after giving birth to Frederick, Harriet Bailey had to return to her work twelve miles away as a field hand. So Frederick was raised by his grandparents. Grandfather Isaac was a carpenter and Grandmother Betsy took care of Frederick and any other grandchildren who were in the cabin at the time. "Grandmammy was, indeed, at the time, all the world to me," Frederick later wrote.[3] He observed early on how much his grandmother was respected by her neighbors. She was a good nurse and a fine fisher. She made skillful nets for catching shad and herring, and the boy's early memories were of watching his grandmother standing waist deep in water for many hours hauling in nets full of fish. Frederick's grandmother was also an outstanding farmer. The sweet potato seedlings she planted did so well that her neighbors asked her to plant their gardens along with her own.

Frederick later remembered a happy childhood in his grandparents' cabin. He recalled swinging from the loft where he slept with his cousins, splashing in the nearby sea, and mimicking the sounds of the farm animals. He wrote of a "spirited, joyous, uproarious and happy childhood."[4]

The family lived in an old cabin with a rail floor upstairs and a clay floor downstairs. There was a chimney but no windows. A hole in front of the fireplace was used to protect sweet potatoes from the frost. Though Frederick spent happy hours tending the garden and chasing squirrels, he described a shadow that always darkened his world. He knew that somewhere there was a white man who owned him and his grandmother.

Although Frederick said that he saw his mother only "four or five times," in his whole life, he wrote vividly of her.[5] "She was tall and finely proportioned; of deep black, glossy complexion."[6]

When Frederick's mother came for one of her infrequent visits, she had to walk the twelve miles at night, so she could make the round-trip and be back at her chores in the morning. Because she had to get started for home soon after she arrived, Frederick saw her only briefly and then only in the darkness. He never saw his mother's face in daylight. When she arrived in the cabin, Frederick would be in bed and his mother would lie down with him and comfort him until he fell asleep. They would not speak to each other and when Frederick awoke in the mornings, she was long gone.

Frederick lamented later that he was not "very deeply attached" to his mother.[7] He bitterly resented the slave system for denying his mother the "intelligent smiles of her child."[8]

Frederick had five brothers and sisters. Perry, Sarah, and Eliza were older, and he had little contact with them as a young child. They had been sent away when they grew old enough to do useful work. Kitty and Arianna were born after Frederick, and he knew them until he was six and was himself sent away.

Frederick loved the old cabin where he lived with

At slave auctions, mothers and their children were often separated and sold to different masters.

his grandparents. He could work the well by himself, getting a drink whenever he needed one. He enjoyed watching the ponderous mill wheel turn and seeing all the neighbors come to get their corn ground. But when he turned six, Frederick's world changed dramatically. His sister Kitty was only four and Arianna was two when, in the late summer of 1824, Frederick took his grandmother's hand and began a long journey. It was a beautiful morning and Frederick was lighthearted. His grandmother did not tell the boy what would soon happen.

The journey was hard for little Frederick, so his grandmother frequently lifted him to her shoulders and carried him until he felt strong enough to march farther on his own short legs. Frederick described his grandmother as "remarkably straight in figure and elastic and muscular in movement."[9] She wore a smoothly ironed bandanna and when Frederick was frightened by what appeared to be a wild animal peering from the woods, she offered her skirt for him to hide behind.

The woman and child arrived at the beautiful home of Colonel Edward Lloyd. Frederick was sent off to play in a group of black, brown, and copper-colored children. They were all strangers to him. He was told that Perry, his brother, and Eliza and Sarah, his sisters, were among them, but Frederick did not recognize his siblings.

His grandmother patted Frederick on the head and told him to play with his brother and sisters because "they are kin to you."[10] Frederick was troubled by the fact that his grandmother looked terribly sad.[11] He was drawn to play with the other children, but he was nervous about letting go of his beloved grandmother's hand. She was the rock he had always clung to.

Frederick joined the group of playing children and in a little while one of the children shouted, "Fed, Fed, grandmamma gone!"[12] The frantic little boy ran to the kitchen in search of his grandmother. Not finding her there, he rushed outside. He fell on the ground sobbing. Perry came to console him, offering him some peaches and pears. Frederick hurled the fruit to the ground and sobbed until weariness finally overtook him and he fell asleep. He was never again to see his grandmother.

When Frederick recovered from the loss of his grandmother, he began to survey his new surroundings. Wye House, the center of Colonel Lloyd's plantation, was a lavish place surrounded by broad green lawns, magnificent gardens, and orange trees. Elegant carriages came and went, bringing well-dressed ladies and gentlemen to elaborate feasts. Edward Lloyd was one of the richest men in Maryland. The small boy, accustomed to simple, plain food, saw for the first time in his life slabs of fragrant cheeses, golden butter, wild geese and partridges, crisp lettuce, figs, raisins, and almonds, all served with brandies, wines, and flavored teas. Frederick later said that all this grand living was "blood bought" on the backs of slaves.[13]

Frederick's master was Aaron Anthony, whose home was on the Lloyd plantation. Anthony managed the estates owned by Colonel Lloyd. Anthony, usually called Captain Bay, owned two or three farms and thirty slaves. Frederick was sent to live in Captain Anthony's house, which was run by a black slave called Aunt Katy. Frederick described her as "ambitious, ill tempered, and cruel."[14]

For the first time in his young life, Frederick learned what it was like to be treated as a slave. He slept on the floor in a closet near the kitchen. No more cozy cabin loft with his cousins. He ate cornmeal mush from an oyster shell or a shingle with the other slave children. They crouched together at a trough like animals. Like all slave children, Frederick had no shoes, stockings, trousers, or jacket. His only clothing was two coarse linen shirts each year that hung below his knees. If these garments fell apart from wear before the year was up, the children went naked. Boys and girls, seven to ten, went naked in summer and winter.

While living on the Lloyd plantation, Frederick received his last visit from his mother. It had been a very bad day for the boy because he had aroused the ire of Aunt Katy, who ruled the kitchen and the children.

She decided to punish Frederick by denying him his evening meal, a slice of cornbread, which he lived for. In fact, Aunt Katy threatened to "starve the life out of" Frederick.[15] Frederick watched the other children getting their ration of cornbread and he went outside and wept. Later, he managed to steal a few kernels of corn. He was nibbling on them when his mother arrived.

Frederick told his mother what had happened and how he was too hungry to sleep. Harriet Bailey marched up to Aunt Katy and scolded her for her cruelty. Then Frederick recalled, "I learned the fact that I was not only a child, but *somebody's* child."[16] His mother brought him a sweet cake in the shape of a heart, with a rich, dark ring glazed at the edge of it. Frederick later recalled eating the little cake and feeling "prouder on my mother's knee than a king upon his throne."[17]

Frederick remembered this night for the rest of his life. It was especially powerful because he never saw his mother again. Harriet Bailey grew very sick and suffered for some time, but the boy was never told of her illness. He was not able to visit her when she was dying, nor did he even learn of her death until some time after it happened. She died in 1825 or 1826, while still a young woman. Frederick later grieved that his mother died alone, without the comfort of her children around her. "The heartless and ghastly form of *slavery* rises between mother and child, even at the bed of death," he wrote.[18]

Frederick's master, Captain Anthony, was a fifty-seven-year-old widower who shared his home with two sons and a daughter. Son Richard was a wastrel, and son Andrew a brutal drunkard. Daughter Lucretia, however, about twenty years old, developed an affection for Frederick. "[She sometimes gave] me a piece of bread and butter," he recalled.[19] She was married to Thomas Auld and had no children of her own. When Aunt Katy deprived Frederick of food, Lucretia would frequently sneak snacks to him.

Although Frederick was forbidden to wander over to Wye House and visit with the slaves there, he could not resist sneaking out to see the wonders there. Frederick met Daniel Lloyd, son of Colonel Lloyd, and a friendship developed between the boys. Daniel was five years older than Frederick, but he had no white playmates so he chose Frederick to go hunting with him in the woods. Daniel shot the birds, and Frederick retrieved them. Frederick treasured his friendship with Daniel and later wrote, "I had two friends, both at important points—Mas' Daniel at the great house, and Miss Lucretia at home."[20]

Daniel Lloyd had a tutor who was teaching him to read and write. During the lessons, Frederick remained nearby, learning too. With his gift for imitating sounds, Frederick repeated the patterns of speech the tutor used. Frederick made a conscious effort to sound like the white people at Wye House. He was always questioning Daniel about their habits, and their lifestyle. Frederick had an endless curiosity. He wanted to know what each glittering dish was meant to hold, and what titles like "governor" and "senator" meant.

But, in spite of his friendship with Daniel and Lucretia, Frederick suffered cruelly in Captain Anthony's house. He was often hungry and cold. He wore the same thin shirt day and night, changing it just once a week. During the winter days enough sunlight warmed one side of the house to keep Frederick comfortable, but nights were miserable.

Frederick wrote later, "I had no bed. The pigs in the pen had leaves, and the horses in the stable had straw, but the children had no beds."[21]

When Frederick lay down to sleep in the closet, the floor was cold and he did not even have a blanket. Sometimes he was able to get an empty cornmeal sack that he crawled into headfirst, with his feet hanging out. His feet became so cracked during those cold nights that he could fit a pen inside the gashes.

Frederick was about eight now and sometimes he wished he were dead.[22] He watched the flying blackbirds and envied them. He was keenly aware of the miserable lives of black slave children in contrast to the pleasant lives of white children. One incident especially drove this point home. Captain Anthony's brutal overseer, Mr. Plummer, stripped a black slave girl and tied her wrists to a rafter. He whipped her with cowskin

Slaves had no rights, and their masters could whip them anytime.

until blood streamed down her back. Frederick was so frightened and horrified that he hid in the closet all day, coming out only at nightfall. The sight of the beaten girl haunted him all his life.

In 1826, Captain Anthony became ill and life changed again for Frederick. Lucretia told Frederick he was being sent to Baltimore. She urged him to clean himself up as much as possible because the people of Baltimore were neat and clean and they would laugh at a dirty little boy. Lucretia promised Frederick his very first pair of trousers. For three days Frederick scrubbed himself in the creek, getting all the dead skin off his feet and knees. He looked forward to his new trousers and a new shirt, and he was glad to be leaving the plantation.

On a Saturday morning, Frederick sailed on the Miles River toward Baltimore, and he arrived on Sunday. One of the shiphands took the nine-year-old boy to his new home—the residence of Hugh and Sophia Auld on Fells Point. Hugh Auld was Thomas Auld's brother.

Frederick watched the front door of the Auld house open, and there stood the Aulds and their two-year-old son, Tommy. Frederick recalled the moment with these words: "I saw what I had never seen before; it was a white face beaming with the most kindly emotions."[23] It was the face of his new mistress, Sophia Auld. Sophia told her small son that this new boy—Freddy—would be looking after him. Frederick was deeply moved and overjoyed.[24]

Later, Frederick credited this move to Baltimore, into the Hugh Auld household, as the defining moment of his young life. He felt that had it not happened, he might never have escaped the cruelty of slavery. He believed that it was a special grace of God that sent him to Sophia Auld, and he wrote, "This good spirit was from God, and to him I offer thanksgiving and praise."[25]

3

LESSONS IN FREEDOM

 rederick wrote of his experiences in the Auld house in Baltimore, "I had been treated as a pig on the plantation. In this house I was treated as a child."[1] Hugh Auld, the boy's new master, was a broad-shouldered shipbuilder. His wife, Sophia, came from a poor family living near St. Michaels. Before her marriage she had worked as a weaver. She was not well educated and did not have the manners Frederick had observed at Wye House, but she could read and often read the Bible, though she struggled over the more difficult words.

"I was utterly astonished at her goodness,"

Frederick recalled.[2] The little boy did not quite know how to act around Sophia Auld. Previously he found he could gain the favor of white people by what he called "crouching servility," but this seemed to upset Sophia Auld.[3] She had never been the mistress of a slave before and the situation was equally new to her. Not knowing how to treat Frederick as a slave, the woman simply regarded him as a mother regards her child. She mothered Frederick and he said he did not look at her as his mistress but as "something more akin to a mother."[4] Sophia would sit with her son Tommy on one knee and a book in hand, and with her other arm she would draw Frederick close and read to both boys at once.

Sophia Auld began to teach Frederick the ABC's. She helped him spell words of three and four letters. Frederick was an eager pupil. He had developed a taste for words while listening to Daniel Lloyd's tutor, and now he was rapidly picking up the skill. But these lessons ended abruptly when Hugh Auld discovered what his wife was doing. He angrily ordered Sophia to stop teaching Frederick at once because education destroyed a slave's usefulness. A slave, Hugh Auld insisted, should know nothing but to obey his master— to do as he is told. Education would spoil the best slave on earth, Auld told his wife, and would lead to nothing but unhappiness for the slave as well. Having tasted something better, the slave would never be content with his lot again.[5]

Frederick knew in his heart that Hugh Auld was right in fearing what education would do. But it was already too late to keep the bright young boy contentedly ignorant. He had glimpsed the stars, and he would never forget their brightness.

Frederick remained in the Hugh Auld household for a year before another change wrenched him away. When Captain Anthony died, he left no will, so his property, including his slaves, was to be divided equally among his three children, Andrew, Richard, and Lucretia Auld. But then Lucretia died, which meant that her share would go to her widower husband, Thomas Auld, Hugh's brother. Frederick was part of the property to be given to Thomas Auld.

In October 1827, nine-year-old Frederick was sent back to Tuckahoe. The little boy was brokenhearted when he had to leave Sophia Auld and Tommy. "We, all three, wept bitterly," Frederick recalled.[6] Once more the inhumanity of slavery was brought home to Frederick. No matter how one bonded with people, the law of slavery could break all ties.

All of Captain Anthony's slaves were assembled at the Tuckahoe farm to be disposed of. Thomas Auld took custody of Frederick and then, to the child's great astonishment and joy, Thomas Auld decided to return him to Baltimore and his brother's household.

After that terrible scare, life returned to normal for Frederick. He lived with Hugh and Sophia Auld for the next five and a half years. It was a strange life for the light-colored slave boy who lived in a house where there were no other slaves, with a mistress who regarded him as almost a son. The Auld family gave Frederick the chance to thrive and blossom in remarkable ways.

Sophia Auld respected her husband's order to stop teaching Frederick, but his thirst for knowledge was so strong that he found other ways to learn. He made friends with neighborhood white boys his age and he used them as his new teachers. Frederick was often sent on errands by Sophia, and he always brought along some bread and a book that he secretly carried from the house. Frederick had gone hungry at Tuckahoe, but food was plentiful in the Auld household and Frederick was free to take an extra loaf. When he met the white boys, who were often hungry, he traded bread for reading lessons. Frederick made fast friends among the "hungry little urchins," as he described them.[7] Even better, when Frederick described the evils of slavery to the boys, they shared his hatred of it and expressed sympathy for the plight of slaves. All his life Frederick remembered those boys from the streets of Baltimore with "gratitude and affection."[8]

Around the Auld house, Sophia sang hymns as she worked. Frederick tumbled around with little Tommy. But when Frederick went down to the shipyards to watch the ships being loaded, his mind turned quickly away from childhood things. Frederick learned the meaning of the word *abolition*. He had been born a slave and as much as he hated his situation, he had never before doubted that he would always be a slave, condemned to a meager and miserable life. But now the possibility of freedom began stirring in his soul. Men were talking seriously about abolishing slavery.

When he was twelve years old, Frederick could read newspapers. He found an article about a speech made by John Quincy Adams presenting the concept of abolishing slavery in the District of Columbia. Another time Frederick got into a conversation with two Irishmen on the wharf. When he described his life at Tuckahoe and how the slaves were abused, the Irishmen said they ought to run away to the North and be free.

Frederick Bailey began to entertain the possibility that he would one day be free. And he could think of little else. For the first time he had powerful hopes that he was not condemned to spend his whole life in slavery.

Frederick began to hang out with a rough-and-tumble group of white boys on the wharf. One day, one of the boys took out a book he had gotten from school and started reading aloud a speech a teacher had assigned. Frederick was fascinated by the marvelous words the boy was spouting. He could not imagine a book full of fine speeches like that. Frederick relied mainly on his

Webster's speller, borrowed from other boys, but now he was determined to get a copy of the speech book.

Managing to save fifty cents earned doing errands, Frederick went to a Baltimore bookstore and purchased a copy of *The Columbian Orator*. It was the first book Frederick had ever owned, and it had a great influence on his life. It was filled with great speeches that Frederick had never heard of before. It opened up a world that the young slave did not know existed.

Frederick found speeches by Cato the Roman and Cicero the Greek. He read a speech William Pitt made to the British Parliament and George Washington's

As a boy, Frederick spent time on the docks along the Baltimore Harbor. There he heard men talking about abolishing slavery.

farewell address to his troops after the American Revolution. Most powerful of all was a speech titled "Slave in Barbary." A group of slaves were being sold in Tunisia, an African country, when suddenly an Irishman jumped to his feet to make a speech on the injustice of slavery. Frederick eagerly read these words and quickly grasped the main idea. Even if a master treats his slaves kindly, the slaves want and deserve their liberty. It is not right for one man to own another. The idea was electrifying to Frederick.

As Frederick continued to enjoy the comfort and freedom of the Hugh Auld household, his former master, Thomas Auld, still officially owned him and could at any time reclaim him. A widower, Thomas Auld had found a new wife, Rowena Hambleton, a cross-tempered woman with the reputation of being very harsh to her slaves. Unlike Thomas Auld's first wife, Lucretia, who had doted on Frederick, Rowena had no such kindly sympathies toward any slave.

Frederick had a cousin, Henny, who had been severely injured in a fire. Her hands were so disfigured that she could not open them; they were unusable fists. She was one of Thomas Auld's slaves and now that she was crippled and useless, he sent her to Hugh Auld. Thomas reasoned that because his brother had the bright and able Frederick, it was only fair that he also bear the burden of the crippled Henny. But Sophia found it very difficult to deal with Henny and sent the

Many white Americans, like William Lloyd Garrison,
believed that slavery was wrong.

girl back to Thomas Auld. He was so angered by this that he decided if his brother would not keep Henny, then he should not have Frederick either.

So in March 1833, fifteen-year-old Frederick Bailey was reclaimed by Thomas Auld. He was sent back to the port of St. Michaels, where Thomas Auld fully expected him to be a strong, capable, and obedient young slave fit for any work he was assigned. Auld did not know about the great change that had taken place in Frederick's mind and heart.

Frederick stood on the ship returning him to Thomas Auld's custody, taking close note of the steamships moving toward Philadelphia. That was the direction of freedom. Frederick was now entertaining serious ideas about fleeing north to freedom.

And the word *abolition* continued to stir the boy's soul. Only two years earlier, a man named William Lloyd Garrison had published the first issue of his antislavery newspaper, *The Liberator*. In December 1833, the same year Frederick Bailey was sent back to Thomas Auld, a national abolitionist society was formed in Philadelphia—the American Anti-Slavery Society.

Change was in the air. And change was in young Frederick's heart.

4

THE TURNING POINT

 eenager Frederick Bailey came to the door of Thomas Auld's home in St. Michaels not quite sure what to expect. His friend Lucretia was dead, leaving a small child, Amanda. Thomas Auld's new wife, Rowena, was in charge, and she quickly let Frederick know where he stood. When Frederick responded warmly to the greeting given him by Amanda, Rowena Auld scolded him for showing too much familiarity with his master's family. Frederick had forgotten his place—that of subservient slave. Frederick saw that Thomas Auld's expression was as stern as his wife's.

While in Baltimore, Frederick had attended a number of religious revivals and had experienced a personal religious conversion. His new religious spirit was still very much alive in him, and he hoped that somehow he could convert Thomas Auld to the same beliefs. Surely, Frederick thought, if Auld had a religious conversion too, he would see that slavery was incompatible with true Christianity.

After only three weeks in his new home, Frederick attended a weeklong camp meeting at Bay Side. The revival was open to both blacks and whites. Hundreds of seats were arranged in a half circle in stately tents. There were no seats for the black attendees, who had to stand in a fenced-off area behind the altar. Thomas Auld came to the revival and Frederick had high hopes that Auld would have a spiritual awakening. Frederick hoped Auld would throw himself onto his knees in the straw-filled pit and repent of being a slave owner. Although Thomas Auld did pray more after attending the revival, he still appeared to see no contradiction between his faith and slavery.

Frederick was disappointed, but his own spiritual fires burned brightly. He decided to start a Sabbath school near where he lived for other young black men to gather and teach the gospel to black children. The makeshift school had only a few spelling books and Bibles, but the young men Frederick recruited were fervent. They started the school with about twenty children. Frederick was thrilled by the project. "Here, thought I, is something worth living for," Frederick recalled. "Here is an excellent chance for usefulness."[1]

If Frederick entertained any frail hopes that Thomas Auld's attitudes had been softened by the camp meeting, he was soon to have them shattered. One Sunday, as Frederick and the other young men taught the children, Thomas Auld and some of his white neighbors burst in, wielding sticks. They ordered everyone out. Auld sternly warned Frederick never again to attempt to teach black children anything.

Frederick grew more and more discouraged with his master and despaired of his religious conversion when Auld whipped Frederick's disabled cousin, Henny, and then "set her adrift to take care of herself."[2] Frederick feared the girl would not survive on her own. Auld's lack of compassion also undermined Frederick's faith in organized religion. Thomas Auld was a member in good standing of the Southern Methodist Church, a fact that scandalized Frederick.

Life in the Auld house was unpleasant for Frederick. Rowena Auld was a stingy woman and the slaves often went hungry. Frederick's sister Eliza, also living in the Auld home, taught Frederick ways he could frustrate and annoy their white masters without incurring punishment for outright defiance. Eliza told Frederick to forget instructions, misplace tools, perform tasks badly, and pretend ignorance of the correct procedures. This was a form of slave rebellion that frustrated the master but did not often bring a whipping down on the slave. Rowena Auld, irked by the inept performances of Frederick and Eliza, tried to starve them into doing better. Cornmeal was the only food allowed the slaves, but Frederick and Eliza were not given enough to stave off starvation. This forced them to beg from neighbors or to steal. They did both.

Rowena and Thomas Auld grew so disgusted with the uncooperative Frederick that they decided to hire him out to someone who might turn him into a willing slave. They chose Edward Covey for the task. He was a farmer who lived seven miles from St. Michaels. It was while working for Covey that Frederick was stripped and savagely beaten in an effort to break him. It was here that Frederick gained the courage to strike back at his abuser and discovered his own manhood. Over Christmas in 1834, Frederick finished his work for Edward Covey and spent the holidays with the Aulds. In early 1835, Auld hired Frederick out to another farmer, William Freeland.

Freeland was an educated southerner who ran a small farm and was much less harsh than Covey. Freeland had "some feelings of humanity," according to Frederick.[3] He gave his slaves enough to eat and time to eat, not hurrying them through meals so they might return more quickly to work. He demanded good work and he provided the tools necessary to perform the tasks he assigned. Frederick described his treatment at the Freeland farm as "heavenly" compared to life at the Covey farm.[4]

William Freeland owned just two slaves, Henry and John Harris. All the rest were like Frederick, hired out to Freeland by their masters. Frederick quickly became friends with the Harris brothers and secretly began teaching them to read. Other slaves from the surrounding area learned of the Sunday lessons and joined them.

Frederick credited Freeland with being the best master he ever had, but still it was slavery and Frederick yearned to be his own man. Frederick decided that 1835 would be the year he would gain his freedom. He was a tall, strapping seventeen-year-old. He looked like a man and he felt like a man. So Frederick confided to his fellow slaves that he was going to escape, and he invited them to join him. Everyone he talked to seemed interested in the idea, and five slaves, including Frederick, devised a plan. A free black man named Sandy Jenkins befriended the group and shared in their discussions about the escape, but he did not want to take an active part in it.

The five planned to get a large canoe belonging to a nearby farmer on the Saturday night before the Easter holidays and then to paddle up Chesapeake Bay to its head about eighty miles away. They would then turn the canoe adrift, follow the North Star beyond the limits of Maryland, and slip unseen into free Pennsylvania. As an extra precaution, Frederick wrote passes for himself and the others, forging the name of William Hamilton on the passes. Hamilton was the master of one of the five slaves. The passes indicated that the men were traveling with the permission of Hamilton.

On Saturday, the five went to breakfast as usual, though Frederick had a feeling that something was wrong. He had a strong premonition that they had

$200 Reward.

RANAWAY from the subscriber, on the night of Thursday, the 30th of Sepember,

FIVE NEGRO SLAVES,

To-wit : one Negro man, his wife, and three children.

The man is a black negro, full height, very erect, his face a little thin. He is about forty years of age, and calls himself *Washington Reed*, and is known by the name of Washington. He is probably well dressed, possibly takes with him an ivory headed cane, and is of good address. Several of his teeth are gone.

Mary, his wife, is about thirty years of age, a bright mulatto woman, and quite stout and strong.

The oldest of the children is a boy, of the name of FIELDING, twelve years of age, a dark mulatto, with heavy eyelids. He probably wore a new cloth cap.

MATILDA, the second child, is a girl, six years of age, rather a dark mulatto, but a bright and smart looking child.

MALCOLM, the youngest, is a boy, four years old, a lighter mulatto than the last, and about equally as bright. He probably also wore a cloth cap. If examined, he will be found to have a swelling at the navel.

Washington and Mary have lived at or near St. Louis, with the subscriber, for about 15 years.

It is supposed that they are making their way to Chicago, and that a white man accompanies them, that they will travel chiefly at night, and most probably in a covered wagon.

A reward of $150 will be paid for their apprehension, so that I can get them, if taken within one hundred miles of St. Louis, and $200 if taken beyond that, and secured so that I can get them, and other reasonable additional charges, if delivered to the subscriber, or to THOMAS ALLEN, Esq., at St. Louis, Mo. The above negroes, for the last few years, have been in possession of Thomas Allen, Esq., of St. Louis.

WM. RUSSELL.

ST. LOUIS, Oct. 1, 1847.

Slave owners offered rewards for runaways. This poster describes a whole family of slaves that escaped in 1847.

already been betrayed.[5] As the men ate their breakfast, mounted white constables came galloping up. Within minutes, the five slaves were surrounded and placed under arrest. William Freeland's mother, Betsy Freeland, glared at Frederick and screamed, "You devil! You yellow devil!"[6] Trusting her own slaves, the Harris brothers, as incapable of such plotting, she believed rightly that Frederick was the mastermind who had lured the brothers into making plans to escape.

Frederick and the other four were taken to Thomas Auld's store in St. Michaels for questioning. All the slaves denied any scheming. But it was obvious that someone had betrayed them, giving detailed information. Frederick suspected Sandy Jenkins because he was the only person beside the five who knew the whole plan.

Some of the white men gathered in Auld's store suggested the five slaves should be hanged at once for the crime of slave rebellion, but Thomas Auld insisted that they be sent to jail while their fates were decided. The five were tied behind horses and forced to walk fifteen miles to Easton, Maryland. They often stumbled and had to scramble to get back on their feet to avoid being dragged by the horses.

In Easton, the five were placed in jail cells while slave traders gathered outside, eager for the chance to buy the men and sell them south to Georgia,

Louisiana, or Alabama. Frederick was frightened by that prospect, describing being sold south as "a life of living death beset with the innumerable horrors of the cotton field and the sugar plantation."[7]

Frederick Bailey had now been branded as a dangerous slave who had organized others into a rebellion. Rowena Auld urged her husband to sell Frederick and use the money to help buy the new house she wanted. Auld was under a lot of pressure and he walked the floor all night trying to decide what to do about Frederick.

Historian William S. McFeely offers the opinion that Auld "cared immensely" for the boy in his "clumsy, tormented way," and could not bear to send Frederick south into dreadful slavery.[8] What actually happened gives credence to this theory. Auld went to the jail and told everyone, including Frederick, that he was selling the boy to a friend in Alabama. The youth believed he was doomed. But when they were alone, Auld told Frederick that he was not going south after all. Instead, Frederick would return to Hugh Auld in Baltimore, where he would learn to be a skilled tradesman. Auld promised Frederick that if he worked hard and stayed out of trouble, he would receive his freedom at the age of twenty-five.

Thomas Auld's remarkable act of compassion had spared Frederick a terrible fate, but the young man had no intention of waiting another eight years for his freedom.

5

DREAM OF FREEDOM FULFILLED

rederick arrived at the Auld house on Philpot Street in Baltimore, but everything had changed. He was now eighteen, fully a man. He had worked as a field hand and had attempted to escape and been in jail. He was no longer the young boy who once lived in this household. Even Sophia Auld treated him differently. She seemed uneasy in the presence of a grown black man. Little Tommy was now a teenager and he no longer wanted a black older brother.

Hugh Auld arranged for Frederick to serve as an apprentice caulker in the shipbuilding trade, at

William Gardiner's shipyard. The caulker's job was to stop up the seams of a ship to prevent leakage. There was a great deal of prejudice against black workers in the docks in 1836 when Frederick Bailey went to work. He and the other black apprentices were constantly harassed by the white workers and forced to run errands for them. The orders shouted at Bailey and his

Frederick began learning about the ideas of freedom and equality by reading books and newspapers.

black colleagues were usually accompanied by racial slurs. The young white apprentices were especially vicious because they resented competition from black youths. Some of the white boys said openly that the black apprentices "ought to be killed."[1]

One day a white apprentice, Ned Hays, became angry at Bailey and attacked him with a razor-sharp adze, a hatchetlike tool. Bailey defended himself with a heavy wooden hammer, knocking the adze from Hays's hand. Later on, Hays and three of his white friends cornered Bailey. One came from the front, one from each side, and one sneaked up from behind. Bailey was struck on the head with a heavy hand spike. Stunned by the blow, Bailey fell to the ground while the four white men joined in beating and kicking him. When Bailey tried to scramble to his feet, one of them kicked him so hard in the face with his boot that Bailey feared his left eyeball had burst. Bailey's eye closed and blood streamed down his face.

About fifty white workers stood around while this brutal attack took place, and not one of them tried to help the outnumbered black youth. Some of the men egged the attackers on, chanting, "Kill him, kill him. . . . He struck a white person! Knock his brains out!"[2]

Bloody and battered, Bailey finally got to his feet and staggered to the Auld house. When Sophia Auld saw him, all her coolness toward him disappeared. Seeing the young man's swollen, bleeding face, she wept. She hurried to get water and linen and she washed his face. Then she bandaged his head and covered his wounded left eye with a piece of fresh beef, the remedy at that time for an injured eye.

Hugh Auld, hearing of the attack, "poured curses on the heads of the whole shipyard company."[3] He tried to press charges against them and was enraged when he was told that because all the witnesses to the incident were white and none would verify Bailey's story, it was useless to pursue charges.

Hugh Auld took Bailey out of the Gardiner shipyard and Sophia Auld tended his wounds until he was healed. Then Bailey went to work at another shipyard, earning $6 to $7 a week. The entire sum went to Hugh Auld, and this rankled Bailey. He worked hard for that money and he saw no justice in giving it all to Auld.

In the spring of 1838, twenty-year-old Frederick Bailey asked Auld for permission to provide his own room and board and keep some of his wages for himself. Auld agreed to accept a weekly sum of $3, with Bailey keeping the rest and taking care of his own needs, including buying his own caulking tools.

Bailey was both excited and frightened at the prospect of being on his own. He had never before been responsible for his own upkeep. He went frantically in search of as much work as he could do. He was "ready to work by night as well as by day," he later recalled.[4]

Bailey took whatever work was available. He was a butler in the home of a stockbroker for a while, and one of his duties was taking the stockbroker's child to the E.M.P. Wells School, run by Elizabeth Wells on Caroline Street. Working at the school at the time was a free young black woman, Anna Murray. Full lipped and full figured, Murray was darker than Bailey, with large, soft eyes. The two became friends. At the time Bailey was learning to play the violin, and Anna Murray encouraged him. Very soon they were courting. Murray, born in 1813, was five years older than Bailey. She was one of twelve children of Mary and Bambarra Murray, a family living on the far side of Tuckahoe Creek near the town of Denton in Caroline County, Maryland. Murray's parents were freed from slavery one month before their daughter's birth, so she was born free. At the age of seventeen, Murray had begun working as a domestic for Baltimore's white families, and she had the reputation of being a fine housekeeper.

Bailey recalled the comfortable family life he had shared in the Hugh Auld household, and he longed for a family of his own. Very early in their courtship, the young couple began making plans for marriage and saving money for their future together. Though she earned low wages, Murray managed to put aside a little each week, and Bailey saved diligently from the $6 he kept weekly. When the couple married, Bailey would remain a slave, but because Murray was a free woman, all the children of the union would be born free.

Since Bailey was planning to get married and start his family, he was more determined than ever to put slavery behind him. He had to make his escape quickly. One day, just before dawn, Bailey obtained the papers of a free seaman, purchasing them with his savings. On September 3, 1838, Bailey donned a red shirt, knotted a handkerchief around his neck, and placed a flat-topped broad-brimmed sailor's hat on his head. He climbed into a carriage driven by a friend and was taken to the train station. He had the address of a friend who would help him in New York and a bag containing his few possessions. But Bailey did not have a ticket. He jumped aboard the train and when the conductor came around, Bailey showed his seaman's paper and some cash. At Havre de Grace, Maryland, Bailey left the train and boarded a ferry to cross the Susquehanna River. He boarded another train at Wilmington, Delaware, and then took a steamboat for Philadelphia. He took a ferry and the night train to New York, and soon he was walking through the crowded streets of the big city. "Dreams of my childhood and the purposes of my manhood were now fulfilled," Bailey recalled thinking as he breathed the free air.[5]

Bailey went to the home of David Ruggles, head of the Vigilance Committee that helped fugitive slaves who had come north. Frederick Bailey had changed his name to confuse any bounty hunters tracking runaway slaves. He called himself Frederick Johnson. Under that name he wrote back to Anna Murray, asking her to join him in New York. Her trip required three trains and four boats between Baltimore and New York, but they had carefully planned everything and soon the young couple was reunited.

Wasting no time, Anna Murray put on a plum-colored silk dress and Frederick donned the good suit he had carried in his bag for just this occasion. They went before James W. C. Pennington, a Presbyterian minister, himself a fugitive slave from Maryland. He pronounced them joined together in holy matrimony on September 15, 1838. With their wedding certificate and a $5 gift from Ruggles, the young couple began their married life.[6]

Frederick and Anna Johnson headed for New Bedford, Massachusetts, to the home of another couple whose last name, by coincidence, was also Johnson. David Ruggles had directed them there. In that house they spent their first night as man and wife. During breakfast the next morning, Frederick decided that his newly adopted last name of Johnson was too common. He wanted a permanent new name. Because of the danger associated with the name Bailey, he could never return to that last name, so he and his host discussed other possible names. The host, Nathan

After he escaped from slavery, Frederick married Anna Murray.

Johnson, had just finished reading Sir Walter Scott's *Lady of the Lake* and he came across a heroic Scottish chieftain named Douglas in the story. Nathan Johnson suggested to his guest that this might be a good choice for him, especially since it was a very noble name belonging to someone who, like Bailey, was brave. After a search of the city directory revealed many people named Douglas, Frederick decided he would adopt the name but make it unique by adding another *s* at the end. Frederick Johnson became Frederick Douglass, a name he kept for the rest of his life.

Frederick Douglass now had a wife and soon there was a baby on the way. He needed to work and he was willing to do anything. His first wages as a married man consisted of two silver half dollars he earned for shoveling a pile of coal into a minister's cellar. Douglass then borrowed a saw from Nathan Johnson and looked for work sawing wood. Douglass wanted something better than woodcutting though. He was bright and ambitious and he did not feel like an unskilled laborer. Still, he had to shovel coal, saw wood, dig cellars, clear rubbish, and load and unload ships to support himself and his wife. Anna Douglass, pregnant, could not work, so their income depended on Frederick Douglass. In the spring of 1839, work became more plentiful. Douglass got a job at a brass foundry and then, at last, as a caulker in the shipyards, a job he was skilled at. On June 24, 1839, the first child was born to the Douglasses—daughter Rosetta.

During 1839, Douglass was regularly reading *The Liberator* and taking its abolitionist message to heart. He deeply admired the editor, William Lloyd Garrison, and he became a subscriber to the paper. Douglass could not afford to pay for the newspaper, but it was offered to him by an agent giving away free subscriptions as a promotion. As Douglass later put it, *The Liberator* "became my meat and . . . drink."[7]

Douglass had never read such thrilling words as he found in Garrison's newspaper. *The Liberator*, Douglass said, contained words "full of holy fire and straight to the point."[8] To the young fugitive slave who had trembled with bitter rage when southern ministers justified slavery as godly, these words that slavery was a sin in the eyes of God were welcome indeed.[9]

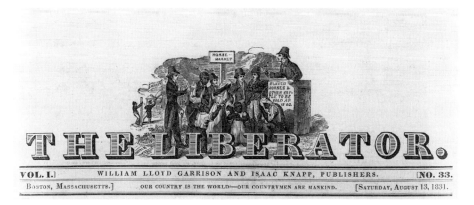

Douglass's anger and ideals were fueled by articles published in *The Liberator*, a newspaper that condemned slavery.

Douglass began attending antislavery meetings in New Bedford. He was content to sit and listen to the rhetoric of others, never imagining he would someday take his place at the podium. On October 9, 1840, the Douglasses' son, Lewis Henry, was born. Douglass was finally making decent wages at the brass foundry and the shipyards. He had two children to support and he worked relentlessly.

In the summer of 1841, Douglass decided to take a break from his heavy work schedule to attend a large antislavery convention on Nantucket, an island off Massachusetts. It had been arranged by William Lloyd Garrison. William C. Coffin, a white bookkeeper at Merchants Bank and a fervent abolitionist, also attended the convention.

Coffin had once visited the New Bedford Zion Methodist Church, where he heard Douglass saying a few words to the congregation about what he had suffered as a slave. Coffin approached Douglass and asked him if he would tell the Nantucket convention what he had told his church group. Twenty-three-year-old Douglass had not minded sharing his experiences with his friends and neighbors at church, but the thought of addressing this large gathering of well-educated people was daunting. Still, he swallowed his fear and stood up to give his first abolitionist lecture.

6

AN ORATOR IS BORN

Frederick Douglass recalled after his speech to the convention that he had stood erect with great difficulty and throughout his presentation he had hesitated and stammered. He was followed at the speakers' platform by William Lloyd Garrison himself, who referred to the eloquent words of the young fugitive slave. Douglass was asked to be a speaker for the antislavery cause. He accepted and was determined to go wherever he was sent. For Anna Douglass, who was carrying their third child, this would mean considerable separation from her husband.

Anna Douglass was illiterate, so there are no letters or other written records of how she felt about her life as the wife of a man who was growing more active in the abolition movement. Many years later her daughter, Rosetta, would describe times of loneliness and frustration for her mother.

Douglass moved the family from New Bedford to Lynn, Massachusetts, a Quaker town a few miles north of Boston. During the next two years, Douglass was always on the go, taking trains to meetings and conventions. While traveling to Dover, New Hampshire, in September 1841, Douglass was ordered out of his train seat and told to go to the "negro car." When he refused, several white men pounced on him and hauled him from his seat. Later, when confronted with the same situation, Douglass again held his ground. He clutched the bolted bench of the train seat and refused to move. He arrived at his destination still sitting in the seat he had first occupied when the journey began.

In his speeches, Douglass not only condemned slavery in the South but also attacked prejudice against black people in the North, such as the kind he had encountered on trains. He denounced the custom of forcing black people to occupy rear seats in public places, even in churches.

Douglass was always deeply offended when bigotry reared its head under the guise of religion. He felt anger against the hypocrisy that permitted white people to spout Christian principles while cruelly abusing their slaves and denying black people their rights. Though bitterly cynical about organized religion, especially as practiced by southern Christians, he maintained throughout his life a strong Christian faith. He made a sharp distinction between his anger against religious people who sanctioned the "bloody atrocities of slavery" and his own beliefs.[1] "I love the religion of our blessed savior," he said. "I love the religion that comes from above in the 'wisdom of God, which is first pure, then peaceable, gentle and easy to be entreated, full of mercy and good fruits.'"[2]

Douglass also believed firmly in his own salvation, writing, "I have no uneasiness about the hereafter. I am in the tradewinds of God. My bark was launched by him, and he is taking it into port."[3]

A bond was forged between Douglass and William Lloyd Garrison at the Nantucket convention. Douglass had revered Garrison even before meeting him, because of Garrison's writings in *The Liberator*. On hearing Garrison speak for the first time, Douglass said, "I saw the deadened hopes of my race resurrected and ascended."[4] During their long relationship, there would be sharp disagreements and eventually a serious rift, but Douglass never lost his deep sense of admiration for and gratitude to Garrison.[5]

In January 1842, only six months after his debut as

a speaker, Douglass had already reached a striking level of eloquence. He was surrounded by giants in the abolition movement when he made a speech at Boston's Faneuil Hall, but Elizabeth Cady Stanton, a leader in the movement to gain the vote for women, said the audience was "completely carried away by the wondrous gifts of his pathos and humor. On this

Elizabeth Cady Stanton, a leader for women's rights, also worked to end slavery. She was impressed by Douglass's "wondrous gifts" as an abolitionist speaker.

occasion, all the other speakers seemed tame after Frederick Douglass."[6]

Douglass was described as having a "rich, melodious voice," and he gazed at the ceiling of the auditorium as he spoke, like a southern preacher staring into the slave galleries in a church while trying to justify slavery.[7] Douglass ridiculed the hypocrisy of such preaching, moving his audience from anger to laughter to tears. But even as he publicly described his own life as a slave, he was still a fugitive slave at risk of being captured and returned to his master in Maryland—Thomas Auld.

At twenty-four, Douglass had not yet reached the age at which Auld had promised freedom for him, and then only if he stayed out of trouble as a faithful slave. Douglass had not fulfilled those conditions.

On March 3, 1842, the Douglasses' third child, Frederick Jr., was born. Anna Douglass, a quiet, reserved woman, was not comfortable in her husband's growing limelight. It was especially intimidating to a woman who could not read to have a husband growing more famous by the day for his great oratory. Anna Douglass knew her husband spent many hours in the company of brilliant men and women who were a far cry from her and her simple ways. The more his world expanded, the more she retreated into their home, immersing herself in their children, her piecework sewing, and her housekeeping.

The year 1843 was called the Year of the Hundred Conventions. There were to be one hundred antislavery conventions organized by the American Anti-Slavery Society. Douglass spoke at most of the meetings, traveling throughout New England, New York, Ohio, Indiana, and Pennsylvania. Not all those speeches were welcomed by gracious audiences.

In Pendleton, Indiana, the meeting was scheduled to be held in a Baptist church, but it was moved when there were threats that the church would be burned down. The meeting was instead held on the steps of the church. A rainstorm interrupted the meeting and it was rescheduled for the following day, amid rumors that white men were planning to cause trouble. The next day found the antislavery meeting taking place in a grove of trees where seats and stands had been brought in. There was a sudden shout and an angry mob of about thirty white men came running from the woods carrying stones and rotten eggs. Some of the speakers were struck with rotten eggs. Men with stinking egg yolk running down their faces did nothing to retaliate.

But Frederick Douglass was not so meek. He grabbed a piece of lumber and began swinging it at the tormentors. This action violated William Lloyd Garrison's strict insistence on total nonviolence no matter the provocation. William A. White, a young white Harvard abolitionist who was Douglass's friend, quickly rushed to stand beside Douglass. When one of the white men swung a club, knocking Douglass to the ground and breaking his right hand, White snatched up a stick to help his friend. Another white man tried to strike Douglass with such a fierce blow to the head that it might have killed him, but White knocked the cudgel from the man's grasp before it reached his target. Someone threw a stone at White and it hit him in the head, causing a gash that bled heavily. Then Douglass and White ran side by side for their lives.

The incident burned itself into Douglass's memory. He was so touched that a young white man like White, who lived a life of ease and luxury, would risk his life to stand by his black friend. When the mob finally dispersed, White lay in the woods, his head gashed and his mouth bleeding from a kick that had dislodged several teeth. Douglass lay nearby, cradling his shattered hand. Later, Douglass's injured hand was not set properly, and it would bother him for the rest of his life.

As Douglass spoke at more and more meetings, some of the people in the audiences began to doubt that he had ever been a slave. He was so eloquent and sounded so well educated that it seemed impossible that he could have been a slave without formal education. When Douglass recounted the harrowing events of his youth, the starvings and the whippings, some listeners shook their heads in disbelief and wondered aloud if this young man was a fraud.

Douglass decided to put to rest all doubts, even though doing so would put his personal safety at risk. He would write a book describing all his experiences, using the true names of all the people who had touched his life, including his masters and mistresses. He would tell everything exactly as it had happened. This was obviously dangerous because he was still a fugitive slave, and once the book was published Thomas Auld would be able to find out where his slave had gone. Douglass decided to take that chance. He felt that the book would make the whole world pay attention to his antislavery message. His crusade would extend far beyond the reach of his voice.

On October 21, 1844, son Charles was born to the Douglass family. They now had four children under the age of five. The following year, fellow abolitionist Wendell Phillips urged Douglass to finish his book, and in his speeches that year Douglass told his audiences that his story would soon be in print for all the world to read.

Though Douglass was a prolific writer, he never left any account of his writing process. When he sat down to write his first book, did he make many drafts? Did he rewrite alone or did his friends help him select what to include and what to omit? It is not known what advice he might have received, nor even who edited the book. At any rate, *The Narrative of the Life of Frederick Douglass, An American Slave, Written by Himself*

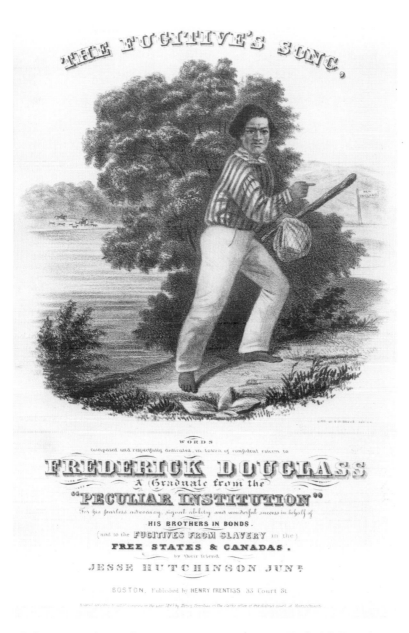

"The Fugitive's Song" was written as a tribute to Frederick Douglass.

was published by the Boston Anti-Slavery Society in 1845. The book tells its readers a lot about slavery, its privations, its cruelty, and how it impacted the life of one man. There are powerful accounts of extreme brutality, but even more affecting are the smaller hurts—the little slave boy denied his meager slice of corn bread, the lonely child huddling in the winter cold in his linen shirt. Only Harriet Beecher Stowe's *Uncle Tom's Cabin* was more influential in revealing the true face of slavery to the American reading public and, eventually, to the world.

William Lloyd Garrison wrote the preface to the book, and Wendell Phillips wrote a letter preceding the text. These famous men lent authenticity to the book. Garrison clearly stated that the book was not ghost-written but came from Douglass himself. The book sold for fifty cents, and by the fall of 1845, forty-five hundred copies were sold in the United States. Within five years, thirty thousand copies had been sold in the United States and Europe. The book became so well known that there could be little doubt that Thomas Auld now knew what had become of Frederick Bailey, his slave.

As the fame of the book spread, Douglass made a trip to Europe to bring the abolitionist message across the seas. The trip also had the advantage of putting Douglass out of Thomas Auld's reach if he sought to recover him. As Douglass sailed to England on the

British ship *Cambria*, he traveled second class but made many friends aboard ship. He gave shipboard lectures on the evils of slavery, winning the admiration and sympathy of many of the passengers. Not everyone was eager to hear his message though. After a fiery speech about the evil merchants who used ships like the *Cambria* to haul slaves from Africa, several angry passengers wanted to toss Douglass overboard. Only the intervention of the captain spared Douglass a plunge into the sea.

While Douglass was away, his wife, Anna, remained in Lynn with their four children. She worked in a shoe factory to keep the family going. Douglass was not making a great deal of money from his book, and his travel in the cause of abolition was expensive. Anna Douglass struggled to do more than her share in his absence.

Frederick Douglass gave many speeches against slavery when he reached Europe, and he also embraced other causes, such as temperance, a movement to induce people to abstain from alcoholic beverages. He gave this message with special enthusiasm in Ireland, where alcohol abuse made the plight of poor families even worse. Observing the misery in Ireland, the thin-armed children and desperate mothers, Douglass was reminded of the plight of slaves in the United States. The potato famine was beginning in Ireland at the time, a famine that would eventually devastate the population and drive vast numbers to relocate in the United States. Douglass wrote a letter to William Lloyd Garrison describing a mud-walled, windowless hut in Ireland with a board on the floor for a table and rags and straw for beds. Between 1845 and 1851, Ireland lost 2 million people to death and emigration.

Douglass made many speeches in Belfast, Ireland, and then went on to Edinburgh, Scotland. For two years he lectured throughout Europe, joined part of the time by Garrison. Douglass was anxious to go back home, but he worried about being captured and returned to slavery. At last, Douglass's English friends raised sufficient money to buy his freedom. In October 1845, Thomas Auld signed a deed of manumission, freeing Douglass for the amount of $711.66. The necessary papers were filed, making Douglass a freed human being on December 12, 1846.

Before leaving Europe, Douglass had discussed starting an antislavery newspaper in the United States. Among those supporting the idea was an English abolitionist, Julia Griffiths, who became a friend and colleague of Douglass's for the next half century.

When Douglass finally returned to the United States on April 20, 1847, he jumped onto the Boston wharf and ran for the train to Lynn. Within fifty yards of his home he was met by two bright-eyed boys, his sons Lewis and Fred, running and dancing with joy.

Douglass took one by the hand and the other in his arms and hurried home.[8]

In the fall of 1847, Douglass began making serious plans for his own antislavery newspaper, an idea William Lloyd Garrison opposed. In order not to compete with *The Liberator* in New England, Douglass moved to Rochester, New York, to live and publish his paper. The Douglass family moved into a two-story brick house, and on December 3, 1847, a four-page issue of *The North Star* was printed. Funds raised in

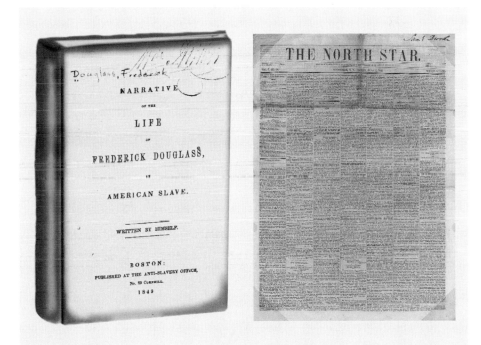

Douglass's first autobiography, published in 1845, was a powerful account of slavery. In 1847, he started *The North Star,* a newspaper filled with articles against slavery.

England to launch the newspaper amounted to $2,001.47. On the masthead of the paper was the motto "God is the Father of us all, and we are all Brethren."[9]

It had been very difficult for Anna Douglass to move to Rochester and give up her familiar surroundings in New Bedford. Daughter Rosetta had been sent to Albany to live and study with two well-known women reform crusaders, Abigail and Lydia Mott. Now, with the family in Rochester, Rosetta would be returning home. It would be hard for the uneducated mother to exert authority over her much more educated daughter.

Because Anna Douglass could not fully share her husband's public life, she took comfort in household tasks and her beloved garden. She never felt comfortable with her husband's literate, often famous friends. She greeted them all at her home with unfailing grace, then withdrew quickly to the kitchen.

Ten-year-old Rosetta was a student in Miss Lucilia Tracy's school in Rochester, and Douglass was getting good reports on her progress. But when Douglass asked his daughter how she was doing, she wept and admitted she was kept separate from the white students. Douglass described himself as "shocked, grieved, and indignant" by the fact that Rosetta was studying "in a room by herself."[10] When Douglass complained to the school, Tracy polled the children to see if they would accept a black student among them. The children all agreed that they wanted Rosetta with them, but one white father protested having a black child study with his daughter. Rosetta was given her pencils and books and told to go home. Frederick Douglass sent his daughter to another school, but he was deeply hurt by the incident.

On March 22, 1849, the Douglasses' fifth and last child, Annie, was born. Soon after that, Julia Griffiths, Frederick Douglass's friend from England, arrived at the family home. She had contributed money to launching *The North Star*, and now she came to help straighten out the financial state of the paper. Though well received, *The North Star* was costly to print and its target audience, black people, often lacked the funds to subscribe.

Douglass had been forced to mortgage his home to keep the newspaper going, and he had written to Griffiths of his troubles. She came immediately and put *The North Star* back on track financially. The mortgage loan was paid off and revenue from the paper was helping to support the Douglass family by 1851. But there was considerable gossip concerning the relationship between Frederick Douglass and Julia Griffiths. The two worked together constantly, and when Douglass went on speaking tours he was often accompanied by Griffiths and her sister. Eyebrows were raised at the sight of a black man escorting two white ladies. After attending a New York City convention, Douglass and the sisters were confronted by a mob of white men shouting obscenities. Douglass was dragged away and beaten until the sisters found a white police officer to come to his rescue and drive the attackers away.

Julia Griffiths had a friendly relationship with Anna Douglass in the house the women shared. Griffiths even tried to teach Anna Douglass to read, but she failed in the effort. Though Anna Douglass apparently made no objection to the unusual situation of another woman living with the family, gossip became so intense that Griffiths moved out of the Douglass home. However, Julia Griffiths remained a close associate of Douglass in their shared antislavery crusade. In 1855 she returned to England, but she and Douglass continued to write to each other for the next forty years.

In 1851, Douglass was contacted by another famous woman, Harriet Beecher Stowe, an abolitionist author who was in the process of writing a dramatic novel about slavery—*Uncle Tom's Cabin*. Douglass and Stowe discussed the problems of slaves who came north without skills enough to survive. Douglass shared with her his dream of a manual arts school near Erie, Pennsylvania, that would help needy and uneducated black youths learn a trade. Stowe, however, doubted that "the coloured population has advanced sufficiently to carry it through."[11] The dream died for lack of funds.

In June 1851, Douglass replaced *The North Star* with another newspaper, *Frederick Douglass's Paper*. Momentous events were taking place in the United States that were having a great impact on slavery. The 1850 Missouri Compromise contained the Fugitive Slave Act, which greatly strengthened the reach of slave catchers. Runaway slaves could be more easily hunted down on northern streets and forced back to their southern masters. Douglass became even more deeply involved in the Underground Railroad, a system of safe houses that sheltered escaping slaves as they traveled from the South to the North. Canada was the only truly safe refuge from slave catchers now. During the 1850s, the Douglass house became a safe house, offering a haven to runaway slaves. Douglass became a superintendent on the Underground Railroad, taking charge of arranging the establishment of safe houses where runaways could get food and shelter on their way to freedom. At times, a dozen slaves hid in the Douglass home. Frederick and Anna Douglass fed, housed, and comforted hundreds of fleeing men, women, and children.

Douglass quickly attacked the Fugitive Slave Act in newspaper articles and speeches, and his oratory against slavery became more bitter. In a speech on July 4, 1852, he used the occasion of the nation's Independence Day to point to the horror of slavery. He called the festive celebration of freedom on this day "a sham" to black Americans.[12] He closed with a dire warning. "A horrible reptile is coiled up in your nation's bosom," he cried. *"For the love of God, tear away* and fling from you the hideous monster *and let the weight of twenty millions crush and destroy it forever!"*[13] This speech has been called the "greatest antislavery oration ever given."[14]

In 1855, Douglass published his second autobiographical book, *My Bondage and My Freedom*. It provides an even deeper and more insightful look at slavery than his *Narrative* does.

The rift between Douglass and William Lloyd Garrison was growing deeper. Though both of them hated slavery with a passion, they had very different ideas about how best to fight it. Mutual friends lamented the bitterness between the two men and believed it harmed the entire abolition movement.

7

FIGHTING FOR FREEDOM

arriet Beecher Stowe criticized William Lloyd Garrison for his anger toward Frederick Douglass. She scolded him for speaking of Douglass as an "apostate" who had given up his principles.[1] Stowe, along with many other abolitionists, feared the harm disunity was doing to the movement.

But the disagreements were too real to be papered over. Garrison fervently believed that violence was never an option. In 1849, Frederick Douglass was telling audiences that a slave revolt might be necessary to end slavery. Garrison saw the United States Constitution as

In her novel *Uncle Tom's Cabin,* Harriet Beecher Stowe exposed the hardships of slavery.

a proslavery document that could never be used to serve the goals of abolition. Garrison called the Constitution "a covenant with death and an agreement with hell" and publicly burned the document to make his point.[2] Douglass wanted to make political appeals for abolition that would use the principles within the Constitution. The only means Garrison saw to end slavery was to convince people that it was morally wrong. Douglass feared that Americans could never be convinced by moral appeals to their better natures. With such deep differences, the two men could not reconcile.

In 1857, the United States Supreme Court affirmed the right of a slave owner to reclaim his slave even if the slave had fled to a free part of the country and now lived there. This decision in the *Dred Scott* case enraged Douglass and he called it "devilish," vowing that it would not stand.[3]

During the 1840s, Douglass had met with a fiery white abolitionist named John Brown. Douglass found in Brown a good friend because of his passionate hatred of slavery. During the 1850s, Brown was a frequent visitor at the Douglass home. In 1859, Brown laid plans to lead an attack on the northern Virginia town of Harpers Ferry, seize weapons in the federal arsenal, and hold local citizens hostage while he organized a slave rebellion in the area. Brown discussed the plan with Douglass. Douglass was sure it was doomed.

After meeting with Brown and his small group of followers, Douglass grew even more pessimistic about the chances for success in a raid on Harpers Ferry. He told Brown that he was going into "a perfect steel trap" and that he and his men would be blown "sky high."[4] Brown continued to ask for Douglass's help, but Douglass turned him down.

On October 18, 1859, Brown led his army of twenty-two men on Harpers Ferry and seized the arsenal. The next night federal troops led by Colonel Robert E. Lee stormed the armory where Brown and his men were barricaded, capturing Brown, killing one of his sons, and ending the rebellion.

Douglass was lecturing in Philadelphia when he learned of Brown's capture. He also learned that the federal troops found a note from Douglass on one of Brown's men. The governor of Virginia immediately tried to implicate Douglass in the conspiracy against Harpers Ferry. He asked President James Buchanan to assist in arresting all of Brown's allies, including Frederick Douglass. Douglass was to be charged with inciting servile insurrection.

The sheriff of Philadelphia received orders to find Douglass and arrest him. Douglass quickly left Philadelphia and went to New York, but he did not feel safe there, either. He boarded a boat for Canada. It was a prudent move. The next day United States marshals arrived in Rochester looking for him.

John Brown hated slavery, but his plan for a slave rebellion in Harpers Ferry, Virginia, failed miserably.

Douglass had been planning another lecture tour in Europe, so he left Canada for England in November. On December 7, 1859, Douglass received a letter from his daughter Rosetta, telling him that John Brown had been hanged by "Virginia hyenas."[5]

In England Douglass visited with his old friend and associate Julia Griffiths, who had married. Douglass made many speeches against slavery to European supporters, but a personal tragedy turned the triumphant tour into sorrow. While in Glasgow, Scotland, Douglass learned that on March 13, 1860, his bright, spirited younger daughter, Annie, had died just nine days before her eleventh birthday. Anna Douglass was disconsolate. The little girl, her namesake, had been the charming delight of both her parents. Douglass himself had received a cheerful letter from Annie in December describing her adventures at school and her academic progress. Soon after that, she became ill and lost the power to hear or speak. Doctors were unable to diagnose her malady, and she died after lingering for three months. Rosetta Douglass took comfort in the fact that her little sister "has gone to Him whose love is the same for the black as the white."[6] Douglass's grief was made more intense by his regret that he had not been home during Annie's illness. He called her "the light and life of my house."[7]

When Douglass returned to the United States, the presidential election of 1860 was under way. He saw it as crucial in the fight for abolition. He first campaigned for his friend Gerrit Smith, candidate for the Constitutional Union Party, which had a strong antislavery platform. But Douglass soon realized that Smith could not win and that either Abraham Lincoln, the Republican, or Stephen Douglas, the Democrat, would become president. Douglass despised Stephen Douglas as "a most dangerous man," saying further, "No man of his time has done more than he to intensify hatred of the negro."[8] Neither was Douglass a fan of Lincoln, accusing him of being "entirely devoted to the welfare of white men."[9] But Lincoln was the lesser of evils in Douglass's view, so Lincoln got his support.

When Lincoln was elected in November, Douglass was glad, but he grew impatient when the election was not followed by a sharp rise in antislavery sentiment.

On December 3, 1860, Douglass was attending a meeting in Boston's Tremont Temple when a group of proslavery white men entered the building. As Douglass rose to make his speech, the white men barred his way to the podium. Douglass charged toward them, battering his way through their ranks to begin his speech. Douglass thundered against the "outrageous" attack on free speech.[10] His enemies yelled loudly to drown him out and he responded by shouting that some white men of the North would "murder liberty—kill freedom."[11] A general riot ensued. Chairs were hurled onto the stage and

Douglass was finally grabbed by the hair and thrown out of the temple by police.

By the end of 1860, events were moving swiftly, however. Unwilling to accept the fact of Lincoln's election, South Carolina seceded from the Union on December 20. On February 1, 1861, five other Southern states—Mississippi, Florida, Georgia, Alabama, and Louisiana—seceded. On February 4, 1861, a convention of the seceded states formed a new government called the Confederate States of America. Eventually Texas, Virginia, North Carolina, Tennessee, and Arkansas joined as well.

President Buchanan made efforts to persuade the southern states to end the secession, but he took no forceful action. He would be leaving office shortly and the terrible problem would fall to the incoming president, Abraham Lincoln.

When Lincoln took office in March, his inaugural address disappointed Douglass. Lincoln's first priority was to end the secession and restore the Union. He said he would uphold the Fugitive Slave Act and would not interfere with slavery in states where it existed.

But, again, events overtook the reluctance of men to deal with them. On April 12, 1861, Confederate troops attacked Fort Sumter, a federal installation in the harbor of Charleston, South Carolina. The fort surrendered in one day. Lincoln called for troops to put down the rebellion, and North and South prepared for war. The North was fighting to preserve the Union, and the South was fighting for the right to secede from the Union and remain a nation where slavery was permitted. But to Douglass and the other abolitionists, the Civil War was about just one thing—the crusade to end slavery. At once Douglass began his campaign to persuade Lincoln to make the war a moral war against slavery.

Douglass had two major goals as the Civil War began. First he wanted the emancipation of all slaves. Second, he wanted all black men to have the right to enlist in the Union Army. When General John C. Fremont emancipated all the slaves of Confederate sympathizers in Missouri, Lincoln voided the action. When General David Hunter freed blacks in South Carolina, Georgia, and Florida, Lincoln did the same. Lincoln was fearful of moving too fast and ruining all chances of ending the secession through compromise. He also feared alienating other states with southern sympathies. But on April 16, 1862, Lincoln outlawed slavery in the District of Columbia.

As Douglass worked for his cause, troubles at home continued. Daughter Rosetta lamented the difficulty in trying to please both her parents. Anna Douglass was a strict God-fearing woman who insisted that the children read a Bible verse at the table each day.[12] Frederick Douglass was more worldly. He did not share his wife's devotion to organized religion. Worse yet,

Douglass urged President Lincoln to make the Civil War a moral war against slavery.

Anna Douglass was still illiterate in spite of Rosetta's efforts to teach her to read. The Douglass children became "patronizing" to their mother because of her lack of education, Rosetta wrote.[13] Rosetta and her mother often argued, so at twenty-three Rosetta moved to Philadelphia to teach school, hoping to be independent. Even there Rosetta was unhappy because she could not do what her famous father found so easy to do: move comfortably between the white, wealthy world, and the world of most black people. In 1863, Rosetta Douglass married Nathan Sprague and the couple eventually had five daughters.

Now, with the Civil War raging, Lewis Douglass was twenty-two, Frederick Jr. was twenty, and Charles was eighteen. They were all the perfect ages to be soldiers in this great cause. When, in September 1862, President Lincoln promised to issue the Emancipation Proclamation, Douglass increased his demands for the inclusion of black soldiers in the Union Army. Governor John A. Andrew of Massachusetts called for black volunteers for the newly formed Fifty-Fourth Massachusetts Volunteers. Douglass encouraged more than a hundred black men to volunteer, including his son Charles. Lewis Douglass signed up next. Frederick Jr. did not enlist.

Lewis Douglass became the first sergeant major and Charles was a private in Company F. On May 18, 1863, the regiment was presented with its colors, and a proud Frederick Douglass watched his two sons in formation. On May 28, the Fifty-Fourth was cheered as it marched through Boston, new soldiers stepping proudly behind drummer boys. They were greeted by Governor Andrew before they boarded transport ships for Beaufort, South Carolina. Frederick Douglass watched the ship bearing his eldest son to war until it disappeared from view.

Sergeant Major Lewis Douglass was in the first battle, an attack on Fort Wagner on July 18, 1863. "Men fell all around me," he later wrote. "A shell would explode and clear a space of twenty feet." He added, "How I got out of that fight alive I cannot tell."[14] He wrote to his girlfriend, "Remember if I die I die in a good cause."[15]

At Fort Wagner, more than fifteen hundred Union men fell. An observer described "dead men strewn in piles and windows, their bodies horribly mangled . . . detached arms and legs and heads were splattered all about."[16]

For Frederick Douglass, the presence of black troops in the war was bittersweet. He was proud of their service but angry that they were paid less than white soldiers. The black soldiers showed great bravery at Millikens Bend and Fort Wagner, but they were treated differently. Worse, the Confederate Congress passed a law that any black soldier who was captured would be treated not as a prisoner of war but as an insurrectionary slave whose punishment would be death. On July 30, 1863, President Lincoln responded by warning that for every Union soldier of any race killed in violation of the laws of war, a rebel soldier would be executed.

Frederick Douglass was now very eager to meet President Lincoln face-to-face, and this happened in the summer of 1863. When Douglass went to the White House he was aware of what a breakthrough this was. Douglass was immediately impressed by the president. "There was no vain pomp and ceremony about him," Douglass noted.[17] "I at once felt myself in the presence

Frederick Douglass was proud to see black men join the fight for freedom in the Civil War.

of an honest man—one whom I could love, honor and trust without reserve or doubt."[18] "I was impressed with his entire freedom from popular prejudice against the colored race," Douglass wrote.[19]

Douglass left the White House after the meeting convinced of the good will of President Lincoln. But when Douglass asked Secretary of War Edwin Stanton for a military commission for himself, none was forthcoming. Douglass had hoped to become the first black officer in the Union Army, serving mainly in recruitment. The army was apparently not yet ready for a black officer, even one as distinguished as Frederick Douglass.

8

THE STRUGGLE FOR EQUALITY

rederick Douglass's son Charles did not see military action in the Civil War because he had lung trouble. When he was very ill, Douglass appealed to President Lincoln for his discharge. An order came at once. "Let this boy be discharged. A. Lincoln."[1] Douglass was grateful to be relieved of this worry, and he began working for postwar equality for blacks. He argued that there must be "but one great law of liberty, equality and fraternity for all Americans without respect to color."[2]

In May 1864, the Democrats chose the popular General George McClellan to run against Lincoln on a platform urging compromise with the Confederate States to end the war. Frederick Douglass campaigned vigorously for Lincoln's reelection and once again met with the president to discuss the future of black Americans after the war. Lincoln did not immediately embrace Douglass's plan for enfranchisement—giving the right to vote to all black males—but he was moving in what Douglass considered the right direction.

The long and costly war was speeding to a conclusion. General William T. Sherman marched through the South and entered Atlanta. This Union victory helped sweep Lincoln to his second-term victory. Near the end of 1864, the Confederacy was almost crushed.

Douglass was invited to the second inauguration of President Lincoln. When lower government bureaucrats blocked his entry to an evening reception at the White House, Lincoln quickly stepped in and got Douglass into the event. On April 9, 1865, the Civil War ended with the surrender of Confederate general Robert E. Lee to Union general Ulysses S. Grant at Appomattox Court House. When, on April 14, President Lincoln was assassinated, Douglass was in Rochester. He joined other mourners in a service at city hall, saying of the fallen president, "Dying as he did die, by the red hand of violence, taken off without warning, not because of personal hate—for no man who knew Abraham Lincoln could hate him—but because

Union general Ulysses S. Grant led the northern troops to victory in the Civil War.

of his fidelity to union and liberty, he is doubly dear to us, and his memory will be precious forever."[3]

With the end of slavery, Frederick Douglass saw his life's dream fulfilled. He was forty-seven years old, strong and still on fire with the cause of black equality. He was eager to help the newly freed slaves adjust to life on their own. Douglass feared the president who succeeded Lincoln, Andrew Johnson, did not share Lincoln's ideals. At Lincoln's inauguration, Douglass had formed a negative opinion of Johnson. When Lincoln pointed Douglass out to Johnson, Douglass believed he saw aversion in Johnson's face. "He is certainly no friend of our race," Douglass believed.[4] When Douglass met with President Johnson to urge him to allow black males to vote, Johnson insisted he had done enough for black people and he wanted to avoid throwing the races together and setting off a race war.[5]

Throughout the South, Andrew Johnson reestablished white governments committed to white supremacy. White landowners reasserted their control over the black population. The Freedmen's Bureau, established in 1865, helped the former slaves with food, clothing, and fuel and allowed them to farm abandoned land. But the bureau was floundering under the mass of freed slaves who were crowded into refugee camps. Death from disease took a terrible toll in the camps. Some weeks, a third of the former slaves staying in the camps died.[6]

Andrew Johnson, who became president after Abraham Lincoln's assassination, was "certainly no friend of our race," said Douglass.

As Douglass was fighting to help his people, his children were establishing themselves in the postwar world. Rosetta Sprague's husband was back from his army service, and the first Douglass grandchild, Annie, was born to the Spragues. Lewis Douglass tried and failed to get a job with the Freedmen's Bureau and eventually found work as a teacher. Charles Douglass tended the family gardens at Rochester. In 1866, Frederick Douglass Jr. and his brother Lewis headed to Denver, Colorado, to seek their fortune in the Red, White and Blue Mining Company. Charles Douglass did finally get a job with the Freedmen's Bureau. Frederick Douglass was offered the job of head of the bureau, but he rejected it because he did not respect President Johnson and did not want to work under him.

In the summer of 1866, the Radical Republican–led Congress, men very sympathetic to freed black slaves, passed two bills favored by Douglass. The Freedmen's Bureau was expanded to provide more assistance to former slaves, and the civil rights bill gave full citizenship to blacks so they would enjoy the rights of other Americans. President Johnson vetoed both bills, but they were passed over his veto. In January 1866, the Thirteenth Amendment declared that neither slavery nor involuntary servitude shall exist in the United States.

Increasingly dominated by Radical Republicans,

Congress passed the Fourteenth Amendment in June 1866 to ensure that rights given black Americans in the Civil Rights Act would be protected by the Constitution. In 1868, the Republicans tried to remove President Johnson by impeachment, but he narrowly avoided removal from office. Frederick Douglass was looking toward the election of 1868 to bring a more sympathetic president into office. He campaigned for General Ulysses Grant, and soon after Grant's election, the Fifteenth Amendment, granting all men, regardless of color, the right to vote, was passed. This caused a rift between Douglass and some of his friends who fought for the right of women to vote. Reformer and antislavery crusader Susan B. Anthony complained that the Fifteenth Amendment placed colored men in the position of tyrants over colored women. When Douglass made a speech saying, "black men first and white women afterwards," there was little applause from Anthony and her fellow campaigners for woman suffrage.[7]

In the South, hate groups like the Ku Klux Klan were terrorizing blacks into submission, and throughout the North, black people faced discrimination. Lewis Douglass had searched in vain for work after he returned from the war, and this enraged his father. Frederick Douglass said of his son, "He had borne himself like a man on the perilous edge of battle. . . . Day after day, week after week, and month after month he sought work, found none, and came home sad and dejected. I had felt the iron of Negro hate before, but the case of this young man gave it a deeper entrance into my soul than ever before."[8]

In September 1870, Frederick Douglass became editor and part owner of the *New National Era*, a newspaper devoted to the cause of black people not as a separate class but as part of all America. Two years later, while Douglass was in Washington, the family home in Rochester burned down, taking many of Douglass's invaluable writings. Nothing was left but ashes. The fire was thought to have been purposely set, but the crime was never solved. What most saddened Douglass was seeing the charred skeletons of trees he had lovingly planted twenty years earlier.[9]

Douglass moved his family to a house in Washington, D.C., and in 1872 campaigned for Grant's reelection. But, in spite of his effort on Grant's behalf, he received no offers of a government job from the Grant administration. Douglass returned to lecturing to earn money. The Douglasses lived in a charming home a few blocks from the Capitol. There were small gardens, but nothing like the large garden Anna Douglass had so loved at the Rochester home.

In March 1874, Frederick Douglass was chosen to be president of Freedman's Savings and Trust Company. It was a national savings bank chartered by the United States. The purpose of the bank was to encourage savings by blacks so they could eventually buy homes and farms. A passbook showing a bank balance was a source of pride to poor former slaves who had never had anything of their own.

Unfortunately, Frederick Douglass did not know the bank was failing when he took the job as president.[10] He was not aware of the generous loans the bank had made that would never be repaid. A financial crisis was gripping the entire United States and many banks were failing. Douglass tried desperately to save the bank, even using his own money to shore it up, and then pleading in vain to the Senate Finance Committee for help.[11] The United States could have bailed out the bank just as it was bankrolling the railroad system at the time, but this was not done. Tragically, many poor black depositors lost the little they had. It was embarrassing and painful to Douglass that he had played a role in an institution that harmed his people.

Another blow struck Douglass in 1874. The *New National Era* could not attract enough subscribers and it closed down in October. Personal and financial problems dogged Douglass. Rosetta and Nathan Sprague were being hounded by creditors and were forced to watch their household possessions being carried off. The other Douglass children were struggling too and were always asking their father for help. Douglass did the best he could, but he was not wealthy.

Douglass campaigned for Rutherford Hayes in the 1876 election. After Hayes was elected, he appointed Douglass marshal of the District of Columbia. It was a largely ceremonial job, but it did give Douglass a large staff of employees to help oversee the criminal justice system in Washington, D.C. He could help black people seeking civil service jobs, and he was able to live more comfortably now that he had a dependable salary. The negative side of all this was that many of Douglass's black friends criticized him for working for President Hayes, who had stopped significant federal action in the South to help blacks. The advances made by the Radical Republicans in the Grant years did not continue under Hayes. There was a return to the old pattern of whites controlling society, and many of the black officeholders elected in the South after the Civil War were now being replaced by white men. New laws, known as Jim Crow laws, were being enacted all over the South, denying blacks equality in jobs, housing, and public accommodations.

There were even charges that Frederick Douglass himself was not allowed to stand beside the president at formal receptions, as the marshal usually did, because of his color. Douglass denied that he was slighted, saying he never had reason to believe President Hayes or his amiable wife looked down on him. In fact, Douglass was a frequent sight at White

Douglass, second from left, was the first black U.S. marshal of the District of Columbia.

House social events, appearing very much at home in White House parlors.[12]

In 1877, Frederick Douglass learned that his former master, Thomas Auld, was now feeble and sick. Douglass returned to St. Michaels, Maryland, for an emotional visit with Auld. When Douglass was ushered into Auld's bedroom, the former master greeted the former slave as "Marshal Douglass," and Douglass addressed Auld as he always had, as "Captain Auld." Douglass did not want the stiff politeness to continue, so he told Auld "not *Marshal*, but Frederick to you as formerly."[13] The two men shook hands, and Auld, trembling and weakened by paralysis, wept. He was deeply moved by the occasion and by Douglass's warmth. Douglass noticed how Auld shook and how ill he was. Later Douglass recalled feeling "choked" and "speechless."[14] Still, Auld's mind was very clear and the two men spoke for a long time about the old days.

"Frederick," Auld said, "I always knew you were too smart to be a slave." Then, commenting on Douglass's escape, he said, "Had I been in your place, I would have done as you did."[15] Douglass told Auld that he did not escape from Auld, "but from slavery."[16]

During the meeting, Douglass learned a consoling fact about the fate of his beloved grandmother, Betsy Bailey. Douglass had always believed that Auld abandoned her to die alone. Douglass wrote in his first book that she had been "turned out to die like an old horse."[17] But Auld now assured him that he had taken care of Betsy Bailey until her death. Douglass noted this in later editions of his book.

In 1878, the Douglass family moved into a beautiful home high on a hill in Uniontown, east of the Anacostia River. The house sat on nine acres with a barn and a large vegetable and flower garden just like the one the family had in Rochester. Anna Douglass once more had a garden to delight in. The following year, Douglass bought an adjacent fifteen acres and the Douglass family settled in at Cedar Hill.

Cedar Hill, the Douglass home in Washington, D.C., is now open as a museum.

9

SORROW AND SUNSHINE

he white frame house on Cedar Hill provided Frederick Douglass with his own spacious library and a music room where his violin rested on the piano. There was a sitting room, guest rooms, and a grand master bedroom. From the large porch, Douglass could look down and see the entire city of Washington. Cedar Hill was a place of pride for Douglass. Walking home in the afternoon, over the bridge and up the hill, the sixty-year-old former slave, who used to beg for crumbs and crawl into cotton sacks to keep warm, knew he had come a great distance in his life.

But his financial woes continued. Douglass was now supporting his own family, his daughter's family, and his son Charles's family. When Douglass's brother Perry and his large family needed help, Frederick Douglass took on their care as well. Now, in 1879, Perry was dying. "He is a dear old fellow," Douglass said, "and I am glad to have a shelter for him."[1]

Anna Douglass's health began to fail as she reached the age of sixty-five. She suffered from a neurological problem that made her unsteady on her feet. She sometimes fell and had to be helped to a couch. She suffered as well from her husband's long absences. Even now, Douglass's attention was distracted from his ailing wife by the controversy over the Exodusters, poor blacks who were leaving the South in great numbers to try their luck in Kansas. At least one hundred thousand blacks made the journey in less than two years. Douglass understood their frustration, calling the citizenship granted in the Fourteenth Amendment to blacks "a mockery."[2] But Douglass opposed the exodus, believing blacks should remain in the South and fight for their rights.[3]

Frederick Douglass served as marshal at the 1881 inauguration of President James Garfield. In the same year he published his third book, *Life and Times of Frederick Douglass*. Additional material in this book included the Civil War and Douglass's impression of recent political developments. After Garfield took office, Douglass lost his marshal's job, but was named recorder of deeds for the District of Columbia.

In July 1882, Anna Douglass suffered a paralytic stroke and became critically ill. Douglass described her as "very feeble," and said, "all that Medical skill and good Nursing can do will be done."[4] The Douglass children gathered around their dying mother for the next twelve days. Her left side was paralyzed and Douglass called her continued grasp of life "a marvel."[5] She died on August 4, 1882, at four in the morning, at the age of sixty-nine.

Grief-stricken at the loss of his wife of forty-four years, Douglass and his children took Anna to Rochester for burial. Douglass lamented that in the midst of such sorrow a person had no time for "pride of self importance."[6] Although Douglass had frequently been separated from his wife as he lectured around the country and the world, he was so depressed following her death that his friends feared he was heading for a breakdown. He was placed in the care of a physician, and his friends took him to Poland Springs in Maine to try to cheer him up. Slowly, Douglass was regaining his interest in life.

His mood darkened again after a Supreme Court decision that, according to Douglass, came upon the country like a clap of thunder from a clear sky and "[placed the United States government] on the side of prejudice, proscription and persecution."[7] In the cases, called the civil rights cases, the Court ruled that the owner of a public accommodation could not be forced to serve black patrons. Douglass said, "The heart of humanity sickens in sorrow and writhes in pain" after such a decision.[8] All the justices were Republicans, so the decision was all the sadder for Douglass, who had loyally served the Republican Party for many years.

In his job as recorder of deeds, early in 1882, Douglass hired a new clerk, Helen Pitts. The forty-three-year-old white woman was from New York, the daughter of abolitionist parents. Pitts was a graduate of Mount Holyoke College and had taught at Hampton Institute. Now she lived with an uncle in Uniontown, right next to Cedar Hill. The Pittses and the Douglasses, already neighbors, became friends. Cedar Hill had become a gathering place for intellectual discussions on the issues of the day, and Douglass enjoyed stimulating conversations with Pitts. Invaluable as an assistant, Pitts kept the business of the recorder's office going smoothly when Douglass was off lecturing.

On January 24, 1884, Frederick Douglass appeared at the city hall and paid the $1 fee to obtain a marriage license. He then called for a carriage to take him to Helen Pitts's residence. Pitts, a petite woman with dark eyes and hair, accompanied Douglass to a parsonage attached to the Fifteenth Street Presbyterian Church. The Reverend Francis J. Grimké, minister of the African-American church, performed the marriage ceremony, which was witnessed by the minister's wife and two household members. Pitts later said of the marriage, "Love came to me and I was not afraid to marry the man I loved because of his color."[9]

When forty-five-year-old Pitts and her sixty-six-year-old husband emerged from the parsonage, reporters thronged around them. The couple escaped quickly to the seclusion of Cedar Hill.

The interracial marriage was a shock to many of Douglass's friends and provoked resentment in his children. Rosetta Sprague later recalled that "it was an unhappy time."[10]

After an elegant wedding supper, the newlyweds went to visit Helen Pitts's parents. Her father refused to welcome his black son-in-law into his home.

Douglass's children and many of his black friends saw the marriage to Helen Pitts as a denial of his black heritage. The black newspaper *Weekly News* bluntly said what many were thinking: "Fred Douglass has married a red-head white girl. Goodbye black blood in that family."[11] Douglass realized the marriage would bring such criticism, but he insisted that "there is peace and happiness within."[12] Later Douglass quipped that it proved he was impartial: "In my first marriage I paid a compliment to my mother's race. In the second, to my father's."[13]

In September 1886, the Douglasses set sail for Europe. On September 24, they visited Douglass's old

"I was not afraid to marry the man I loved because of his color," said Helen Pitts. When she became Douglass's second wife, many people were shocked and upset by their interracial marriage.

friend Julia Griffiths Crofts, now widowed. Though they had kept in touch by letters over the years, Douglass had not seen Crofts face-to-face for twenty-six years.

The Douglasses visited London, Paris, and the ruins of Pompeii. They were having such a good time that they extended their trip to Egypt and Greece. Douglass could not help but relate much of what he saw to the experience of black slavery in the United States. In Egypt, he identified with the story of Moses leading his people from slavery and when he saw black workers in Egypt, he was proud of their skill and diligence.[14]

In March 1887, Helen Douglass's mother became very ill. Helen traveled back home to care for her mother at Cedar Hill. Frederick remained in Europe to fulfill his lecture commitments. He then returned home, and in 1888 toured the South to check on the condition of black people. When he saw the broken-down shacks of tenant farmers, they were hauntingly familiar to him. They reminded him of how he had lived as a slave in the South. He found a dispirited population without hope. In Washington, D.C., for the twenty-sixth anniversary of President Lincoln's Emancipation Proclamation, Douglass lashed out against the cruel conditions he had found in the South. He said that the Fourteenth and Fifteenth Amendments were being ignored. Speeches like this helped restore Douglass's reputation with the black people who had begun to doubt his commitment to their causes.

In 1889, Benjamin Harrison, a Republican, became president. Douglass, now seventy-one, hoped that a job in the Harrison administration would come his way. During the first administration of Democratic president Grover Cleveland (1885–1889), he had no such opportunity. Douglass would have gladly taken back his old job as recorder of deeds, but instead he was offered the job of consul general to Haiti. Secretary of State James Blaine went personally to Cedar Hill to offer him the position.

Douglass's friends urged him to reject the job because Harrison was not a true friend to blacks. Also, Douglass's friends feared that the hot, humid climate of Haiti might be hard on Douglass, especially at his age. Even worse, there was political unrest and a potential for violence in Haiti. Frequently politicians were driven from office or killed. His friends did not believe this would be a good place for Frederick Douglass to be.

Haiti was part of the island of Hispaniola discovered by Christopher Columbus in 1492. By the mid-1500s, thousands of black slaves were being brought to Haiti to labor on Spanish plantations. France gained control of Haiti in 1697, and it became France's richest colony in the New World. In 1793, Toussaint L'Ouverture, a freed slave, led other slaves in a revolution that lasted for several years. L'Ouverture was successful and he freed the slaves by overthrowing French rule. Haiti was declared independent in 1804. During the next decades there were many rebellions and periods of unrest, but it remained a black-led nation, the only one in the New World. In 1889, Frederick Douglass and many other black Americans took pride in the fact that former slaves like themselves were the rulers of a country. So, in spite of the misgivings of his friends, Douglass told Secretary Blaine that he would accept the job as consul general to Haiti.

10

HAITI AND THE
FINAL DAYS

elen Douglass was very good-natured about the assignment to Haiti. When she and her husband reached Port-au-Prince in the old Civil War ship *Kearsarge*, she enjoyed the sights and sounds of the country. For his part, Douglass was proud to be minister to this independent black republic.

When the Douglasses arrived in Haiti, a revolution was under way. Two generals—François De Legitime and Florvil Hyppolite—claimed the presidency. Legitime had the support of France, which hoped to reestablish its influence in Haiti. Hyppolite was driven to a northern section of the country, and to prevent his receiving military supplies, the French were blockading Haiti.

President Benjamin Harrison recognized Legitime as the legitimate ruler of Haiti. Hyppolite, however, gained the support of the United States Navy and some gun dealers in New York anxious to sell him arms. When an American gun merchant loaded ten ships with weapons, the U.S. Navy helped him run the French blockade. President Harrison appeared to be supporting both sides. He publicly recognized Legitime, while permitting the arming of Hyppolite. At the time, the United States hoped to establish a naval base at Mole St. Nicholas in the northeastern tip of Haiti and was possibly trying to make friends with whoever would win the revolution.

On October 7, 1889, Hyppolite became president of Haiti after his well-armed soldiers prevailed. A joint fleet of ships from Britain, France, and Germany was allegedly heading for Haiti to demand payment of debts contracted by the Legitime government. Douglass negotiated an agreement to repay the debt, sparing Haiti possible occupation by foreign governments. Then Douglass was caught up in the efforts to establish a U.S. naval base in Haiti. Douglass was assigned to sell the idea to President Hyppolite, but Hyppolite refused to approve it. Douglass respected his decision because he believed in the right of sovereign nations to make such decisions. But newspaper critics of Douglass in the United States blamed Douglass for the failure to secure the naval base, saying he showed too much deference to the black Haitian president.

As Douglass struggled with Haitian politics, he learned that his son Frederick Jr.'s wife, Virginia, was near death and she would leave two small children. Douglass knew his family responsibilities would increase. Helen Douglass grew ill in Haiti, adding to Douglass's stress. And then, Douglass became increasingly offended by the tyrannical policies of President Hyppolite. Douglass witnessed massacres in the streets as Hyppolite struck out against dissent. On July 30, 1891, Frederick Douglass resigned as consul general to Haiti.

In 1892, Douglass was honored to be chosen commissioner of the Republic of Haiti's pavilion at the world's fair celebration, but he was feeling the burden of age. "I am now seventy-five years," he wrote. "My eyes are failing and my hand is not as nimble as it once was."[1]

Douglass continued his passionate interest in civil rights for his black brothers and sisters. He was especially shocked by the rising numbers of lynchings—murder by lawless mobs—of blacks in the South. There were 235 lynchings in 1892 alone, and 3,000 blacks were lynched between 1882 and 1900.[2] Douglass denounced the lynching of three black men in Memphis, Tennessee, saying they had been killed because they had businesses that white men wanted.[3]

At the Republican convention of 1892, Douglass demanded a greater role for the federal government in protecting the lives and rights of black citizens. Though President Harrison made no promises, Douglass supported him. Harrison lost to Democrat Grover Cleveland, and Douglass blamed his lack of support for civil rights for the defeat.

Helen Douglass's family now accepted Douglass and called him "Uncle Fred," but there was never more than stiff politeness between Helen Douglass and Douglass's children. In July 1892, Frederick Douglass Jr., always frail, died. The fifty-year old namesake of his father had been a journalist. Frederick Douglass and his son Lewis helped care for the eleven-year old son, Charley Paul, left behind when Frederick Jr. died.

Frederick Douglass found joy in Haley George, the son of Charles Douglass. The boy sent his grandfather wonderful letters describing his fishing and crabbing adventures. Douglass had always loved nature, and now he rose at five in the morning to walk around the grounds of Cedar Hill admiring the trees and flowers. He drew great pleasure from reading, and his library was filled with the plays of William Shakespeare and the poems of Lord Byron and John Greenleaf Whittier. Douglass still played the violin and he enjoyed string music. He said, "No man can be an enemy of mine who loves the violin."[4] He was delighted when another of son Charles's boys, Joseph, showed promise in the violin.

Frederick Douglass never relented in his continuing crusade to improve the lot of black Americans. He was still active on the lecture circuit and he never rejected an opportunity to strike a blow for equality.

Douglass invited Ida B. Wells, a fellow black crusader for civil rights, to lunch in Boston one day, and when she told him there was a nice restaurant down the street that did not serve black people, the old warrior

Frederick and Helen Douglass on a visit to Niagara Falls.

Two of Douglass's sons—Lewis Henry, left, and Frederick Jr., right—pose with his grandson Joseph Douglass. Joseph became the first African-American concert violinist.

came to life in the heart of Frederick Douglass. He grasped Wells's arm and told her that they would dine at that place this day. The pair walked to the Boston Oyster House, found a table, and sat down as waiters stared at them. When no waiters came to bring menus, the owner of the restaurant recognized Douglass and came over. Soon the two men were chatting and waiters were summoned to take orders. Douglass and Wells had integrated the Boston Oyster House.

On January 9, 1894, Frederick Douglass delivered his last great speech, at the Metropolitan African Methodist Episcopal Church in Washington, D.C. In this speech, "The Lessons of the Hour," he attacked all the means that were being employed to deprive black people of their rights, from lynching men who had been denied fair trials, to literacy tests designed to prevent black men from voting. He denounced persecution of blacks in the South. The speech was eloquent and classic Frederick Douglass—it was the great orator at his best.

On February 20, 1895, Frederick Douglass attended a women's rights meeting with Susan B. Anthony, where giving women the vote was the topic. Douglass was a commanding figure with his strong features and flowing white hair. He was pleased with progress made at the meeting to develop a strategy for gaining the vote for women. When he returned home to Cedar Hill, he was regaling Helen Douglass with details of the day's events when he suddenly crumpled to the floor and died of a massive heart attack.

Douglass's body remained at Cedar Hill for three days. The immediate family congregated in the parlor, where the Reverend Hugh Stevenson conducted Bible readings and prayer. The body was then taken to the Metropolitan African Methodist Episcopal Church to lie in state for four hours. Thousands of black schoolchildren viewed Douglass in the open casket. The services were attended by many ordinary people, white and black, as well as dignitaries such as Supreme Court Justice John Harlan and the entire faculty of Howard University.

After the funeral, Helen Douglass and the three surviving children took Frederick Douglass to Central Church in Rochester, and finally to Mount Hope Cemetery, where he was laid to rest with Anna Douglass, his first wife, and his daughter Annie. There would be a simple gravestone stating only his name and dates of birth and death.

Praise for Douglass came from all over the world upon his death. The North Carolina legislature closed down for the day to honor him. In Massachusetts, Indiana, Illinois, and New York, the legislatures issued formal statements of regret.[5] The New York State Assembly called Douglass "one of the foremost citizens and most striking figures of the Republic."[6] The Pennsylvania Society for Promoting the Abolition of

Runaway slave Frederick Douglass dedicated his life to speaking out for freedom and equality.

Slavery expressed "appreciation of a life that has made grander the history, not only of our country and our lives, but of the world."[7] From the *London Daily News* came this tribute to Douglass: "First to last his was [a] noble life. His own people have lost a father and friend, and all good men have lost a comrade in the fight for the legal emancipation of one race and the spiritual emancipation of all."[8]

American reformer and civil rights advocate Elizabeth Cady Stanton recalled Douglass as "like an African prince, majestic in his wrath as with wit, satire and indignation he graphically described the bitterness of slavery."[9]

Frederick Douglass himself may have written his most fitting epitaph in 1880 when he said that his life "has at times been dark and stormy," but also "remarkably full of sunshine and joy." He acknowledged "warmest gratitude for the allotments of life that have fallen to me," concluding that he had not "lived in vain."[10]

CHRONOLOGY

1818—Frederick Bailey is born in Tuckahoe, Maryland.

1824—Is sent to work as a slave for master Aaron Anthony.

1826—Is sent to Hugh and Sophia Auld in Baltimore.

1838—Escapes to New York and freedom; marries Anna Murray; changes his last name to Douglass.

1841—Makes first antislavery speech.

1845—First book, *Narrative of the Life of Frederick Douglass*, is published.

1847—Becomes publisher of *The North Star*.

1855—*My Bondage and My Freedom* is published.

1870—Becomes editor of *New National Era*.

1874—Becomes president of Freedman's Savings and Trust.

1877—Becomes U.S. marshal for the District of Columbia.

1881—Becomes recorder of deeds, Washington, D.C.; *Life and Times of Frederick Douglass* is published.

1882—Anna Douglass dies.

1884—Marries Helen Pitts.

1889—Becomes U.S. consul general to Haiti.

1895—Dies on February 20 in Washington, D.C.

CHAPTER NOTES

Chapter 1. "I Was a Man Now"

1. Dickson J. Preston, *Young Frederick Douglass, The Maryland Years* (Baltimore, Md.: Johns Hopkins University Press, 1980), p. 121.

2. Ibid.

3. Ibid.

4. Frederick Douglass, *Narrative of the Life of Frederick Douglass, An American Slave* (New York: W. W. Norton & Company, 1997; first published in 1845), p. 48.

5. Frederick Douglass, *Life and Times of Frederick Douglass* (New York: Library of America, 1994; first published in 1881), p. 588.

6. Ibid., p. 590.

7. Gregory P. Lampe, *Frederick Douglass, Freedom's Voice, 1818–1845* (East Lansing, Mich.: Michigan State University Press, 1998), p. 21.

8. *Life and Times*, p. 591.

Chapter 2. Somebody's Child

1. Dickson J. Preston, *Young Frederick Douglass, The Maryland Years* (Baltimore: Johns Hopkins University Press, 1980), p. 23.

2. William S. McFeely, *Frederick Douglass* (New York: W. W. Norton & Company, 1991), p. 8.

3. Frederick Douglass, *My Bondage and My Freedom* (New York: Library of America, 1994; first published in 1855), p. 143.

4. McFeely, p. 8.

5. Frederick Douglass, *Narrative of the Life of Frederick Douglass, An American Slave* (New York: W. W. Norton & Company, 1997; first published in 1845), p. 13.

6. *Bondage*, p. 152.

7. Ibid.

8. Ibid.

9. Preston, p. 38.

10. Ibid., p. 39.

11. Frederick Douglass, *Life and Times of Frederick Douglass* (New York: Library of America, 1994; first published in 1881), p. 480.

12. Preston, p. 39.

13. McFeely, p. 12.

14. Ibid., p. 18.

15. Preston, p. 63.

16. Ibid.

17. Ibid., p. 64.

18. *Bondage*, p. 155.

19. *Life and Times*, p. 519.

20. *Bondage*, p. 207.

21. Barbara Ritchie, *Life and Times of Frederick Douglass* (New York: Thomas Y. Crowell Company, 1966), p. 19.

22. *Narrative*, p. 33.

23. Ibid., p. 27.

24. Preston, p. 84.

25. *Narrative*, p. 28.

Chapter 3. Lessons in Freedom

1. Frederick Douglass, *My Bondage and My Freedom* (New York: Library of America, 1994; first published in 1855), p. 215.

2. Frederick Douglass, *Narrative of the Life of Frederick Douglass, An American Slave* (New York: W. W. Norton & Company, 1997; first published in 1845), p. 28.

3. Ibid.

4. Dickson J. Preston, *Young Frederick Douglass, The Maryland Years* (Baltimore: Johns Hopkins University Press, 1980), p. 86.

5. Ibid., p. 93.

6. *Bondage*, p. 237.

7. *Narrative*, p. 32.

8. Ibid.

Chapter 4. The Turning Point

1. Frederick Douglass, *My Bondage and My Freedom* (New York: Library of America, 1994; first published in 1855), p. 254.

2. Ibid., p. 255.

3. Gregory P. Lampe, *Frederick Douglass, Freedom's Voice, 1818–1845* (East Lansing, Mich.: Michigan State University Press, 1998), p. 21.

4. Frederick Douglass, *Narrative of the Life of Frederick Douglass, An American Slave* (New York: W. W. Norton & Company, 1997; first published in 1845), p. 54.

5. Dickson J. Preston, *Young Frederick Douglass, The Maryland Years* (Baltimore: Johns Hopkins University Press, 1980), p. 136.

6. Ibid., p. 137.

7. *Bondage*, p. 324.

8. William S. McFeely, *Frederick Douglass* (New York: W. W. Norton & Company, 1991), p. 56.

Chapter 5. Dream of Freedom Fulfilled

1. Dickson J. Preston, *Young Frederick Douglass, The Maryland Years* (Baltimore: Johns Hopkins University Press, 1980), p. 144.

2. Ibid., p. 145.

3. Ibid.

4. William S. McFeely, *Frederick Douglass* (New York: W. W. Norton & Company, 1991), p. 65.

5. Gregory P. Lampe, *Frederick Douglass, Freedom's Voice, 1818–1845* (East Lansing, Mich.: Michigan State University Press, 1998), p. 26.

6. Benjamin Quarles, *Frederick Douglass* (Washington, D.C.: Associated Publishing, 1948), p. 9.

7. Lampe, p. 44.

8. Ibid.

9. Ibid.

Chapter 6. An Orator Is Born

1. Barbara Ritchie, *The Mind and Heart of Frederick Douglass* (New York: Thomas Y. Crowell Company, 1968), p. 43.

2. Ibid., p. 45.

3. Benjamin Quarles, *Frederick Douglass* (Washington, D.C.: Associated Publishing, 1948), p. 297.

4. Gregory P. Lampe, *Frederick Douglass, Freedom's Voice, 1818–1845* (East Lansing, Mich.: Michigan State University Press, 1998), p. 43.

5. William S. McFeely, *Frederick Douglass* (New York: W. W. Norton & Company, 1991), p. 95.

6. Ibid., p. 100.

7. John Hope Franklin, *From Slavery to Freedom* (New York: Alfred Knopf, 1994), p. 182.

8. McFeely, p. 145.

9. Frederick Douglass, *Life and Times of Frederick Douglass* (New York: Library of America, 1994; first published in 1881), p. 1058.

10. Ibid., p. 712.

11. Quarles, p. 131.

12. Ritchie, p. 75.

13. Ibid., p. 78.

14. McFeely, p. 173.

Chapter 7. Fighting for Freedom

1. John D. Hedrick, *Harriet Beecher Stowe* (New York: Oxford University Press, 1994), p. 252.

2. Richard Hofstadter, *The United States: The History of a Republic* (Englewood Cliffs, N.J.: Prentice-Hall, Inc., 1967), p. 309.

3. Barbara Ritchie, *The Mind and Heart of Frederick Douglass* (New York: Thomas Y. Crowell Company, 1968), p. 35.

4. Frederick Douglass, *Life and Times of Frederick Douglass* (New York: Library of America, 1994; first published in 1881), p. 759.

5. William S. McFeely, *Frederick Douglass* (New York: W. W. Norton & Company, 1991), p. 203.

6. Ibid., p. 207.

7. Benjamin Quarles, *Frederick Douglass* (Washington, D.C.: Associated Publishing, 1948), p. 109.

8. McFeely, p. 187.

9. Russell Freedman, *Lincoln, A Photobiography* (New York: Houghton Mifflin Company, 1987), p. 5.

10. McFeely, p. 209.

11. Ibid.

12. Quarles, p. 109.

13. Ibid., p. 110.

14. McFeely, p. 226.

15. Ibid.

16. Ibid.

17. *Life and Times*, p. 785.

18. Ibid., p. 786.

19. Freedman, p. 104.

Chapter 8. The Struggle for Equality

1. William S. McFeely, *Frederick Douglass* (New York: W. W. Norton & Company, 1991), p. 230.

2. Barbara Ritchie, *The Mind and Heart of Frederick Douglass* (New York: Thomas Y. Crowell Company, 1968), p. 131.

3. Ibid., p. 143.

4. Frederick Douglass, *Life and Times of Frederick Douglass* (New York: Library of America, 1994; first published in 1881), p. 802.

5. Benjamin Quarles, *Frederick Douglass* (Washington, D.C.: Associated Publishing, 1948), p. 226.

6. Richard Hofstadter, *The United States: The History of a Republic* (Englewood Cliffs, N.J.: Prentice-Hall, Inc., 1967), p. 457.

7. Ida Husted Harper, *The Life and Work of Susan B. Anthony* (Indianapolis, Ind.: Hollenbeck Press, 1898), p. 324.

8. Ritchie, pp. 166–167.

9. McFeely, p. 275.

10. John Hope Franklin, *From Slavery to Freedom* (New York: Alfred Knopf, 1994), p. 237.

11. Ibid.

12. William S. McFeely, *Grant, A Biography* (New York: W. W. Norton & Company, 1981), p. 427.

13. *Life and Times*, p. 876.

14. Ibid., p. 877.

15. Corrine K. Hoexter, *Black Crusader* (New York: Rand McNally Company, 1970), p. 195.

16. Ibid.

17. *Life and Times*, p. 877.

Chapter 9. Sorrow and Sunshine

1. William S. McFeely, *Frederick Douglass* (New York: W. W. Norton & Company, 1991), p. 297.

2. Dick Russell, *Black Genius* (New York: Carroll and Graf Publishing, Inc., 1998), p. 281.

3. Rayford Logan and Irving S. Cohen, *The American Negro* (Boston, Mass.: Houghton Mifflin Company, 1970), pp. 141–142.

4. McFeely, p. 312.

5. Ibid.

6. Ibid.

7. Frederick Douglass, *Life and Times of Frederick Douglass* (New York: Library of America, 1994; first published in 1881), p. 966.

8. Ibid., p. 968.

9. Benjamin Quarles, *Frederick Douglass* (Washington, D.C.: Associated Publishing, 1948), p. 298.

10. Ibid., p. 299.

11. McFeely, p. 320.

12. Quarles, p. 298.

13. Benjamin Quarles, ed., *Frederick Douglass* (Englewood Cliffs, N.J.: Prentice-Hall, 1968), p. 171.

14. McFeely, p. 331.

Chapter 10. Haiti and the Final Days

1. William S. McFeely, *Frederick Douglass* (New York: W. W. Norton & Company, 1991), p. 360.

2. Rayford Logan and Irving S. Cohen, *The American Negro* (Boston, Mass.: Houghton Mifflin Company, 1870), p. 138.

3. McFeely, p. 363.

4. Benjamin Quarles, *Frederick Douglass* (Washington, D.C.: Associated Publishing, 1948), p. 340.

5. Philip S. Foner, *Frederick Douglass* (New York: Citadel Press, 1964), p. 366.

6. Ibid., pp. 366–367.

7. Ibid., p. 367.

8. Ibid., p. 366.

9. McFeely, pp. 382–383.

10. Frederick Douglass, *Life and Times of Frederick Douglass* (New York: The Library of America, 1994; first published in 1881), p. 1045.

FURTHER READING

Douglass, Frederick. *Narrative of the Life of Frederick Douglass, An American Slave*. New York: W. W. Norton & Company, 1997.

——. *My Bondage and My Freedom*. New York: Library of America, 1994.

——. *Life and Times of Frederick Douglass*. New York: Library of America, 1994.

Foner, Philip S. *Frederick Douglass*. New York: Citadel Press, 1994.

Hoexter, Corinne K. *Black Crusader*. New York: Rand McNally Company, 1970.

Lutz, Norma Jean. *Frederick Douglass: Abolitionist and Author*. Broomall, Pa.: Chelsea House, 2000.

Quarles, Benjamin. *Frederick Douglass*. Washington, D.C.: Associated Publishing, 1948.

Russell, Sherman Apt. *Frederick Douglass, Abolitionist Editor*. New York: Chelsea House, 1988.

Weidt, Maryann. *Voice of Freedom: A Story About Frederick Douglass*. The Lerner Publishing Group, 2001.

Internet Addresses

Biography, image gallery, chronology
<www.cr.nps.gov/museum/exhibits/douglass>

Biography, speeches, pictures
<www.frederickdouglass.org/douglass_bio.html>

Overview of Douglass's life, pictures
<www.brightmoments.com/blackhistory/nfdougla.stm>

Detailed biography of Douglass's life and works
<www.history.rochester.edu/class/douglass/HOME.html>

INDEX

Page numbers for photographs are in **boldface** type.